Unstructured Data Classification

Uncertain Nearest Neighbor Decision Rule

Dr. K. Thippeswamy
Dr. Nijaguna G. S.

ELIVA PRESS

ELIVA PRESS

Dr. K. Thippeswamy
Dr. Nijaguna G. S.

According to certain criteria, the classes are identified by using classification techniques, which is considered as data mining tool. When compared with smaller class, the classification results (i.e., accuracy) for bigger class are deviating and the traditional classification procedures provides inaccurate results, which is known as Class Imbalance problem. A class is formed with unequal size, where this type of data is represented and combined as class imbalance data. There are two various categories are presents in class imbalance domain, namely minority (i.e., smaller) and majority (i.e., bigger) classes. The major aim of this research work is to identify the minority class accurately. In this research thesis, two significant methodologies are proposed such as (i) Adaptive-Condensed Nearest Neighbor (ACNN)Algorithm, and (ii) Local Mahalanobis Distance Learning(LMDL) based ACNN algorithm. These methods are significantly improving the imbalanced data classification.

Published by Eliva Press SRL

Address: MD-2060, bd.Cuza-Voda, 1/4, of. 21 Chişinău, Republica Moldova

Email: info@elivapress.com

Website: www.elivapress.com

ISBN: 978-1-63648-049-7

Abstract

According to certain criteria, the classes are identified by using classification techniques, which is considered as data mining tool. When compared with smaller class, the classification results (i.e., accuracy) for bigger class are deviating and the traditional classification procedures provides inaccurate results, which is known as Class Imbalance problem. A class is formed with unequal size, where this type of data are represented and combined as class imbalance data. There are two various categories are presents in class imbalance domain, namely minority (i.e., smaller) and majority (i.e., bigger) classes. The major aim of this research work is to identify the minority class accurately. In this research thesis, two significant methodologies are proposed such as (i) Adaptive-Condensed Nearest Neighbor (ACNN)Algorithm, and (ii) Local Mahalanobis Distance Learning(LMDL) based ACNN algorithm. These methods are significantly improving the imbalanced data classification.

At first, ACNN algorithm used to summarize the training set, finding the most important observations of information, which will be used to classify any imbalance data. The selection of ACNN data reduces the number of comparisons, which will automatically classify a new observation of data points with maximum accuracy. An appropriate point-explicit k are learned using artificial neural system and neighborhood test points' density are used to distribute by ACNN classifier. The performance of ACNN is validated by comparing their results with existing techniques such as K- Nearest Neighbor (KNN), Neural Network (NN), Random Forest (RF), etc. The experiments are conducted on Diabetes and pop-failure the results showed that ACNN achieved 94% and 100% accuracy on those dataset, when compared with KNN technique for imbalance classification.

The original class data distribution is not changes by the proposed LMDL with ACNN technique, where there is no loss of information or unexpected mistakes. The existing conventional technique faces these problems (i.e., some unexpected errors/information loss may happen) due to presence of less instance in majority class or high instance in minority class.Initially, LMDL selects few set of samples, namely prototypes, and understands a Mahalanobis distance metric for every prototype based on a closely related objective function. Furthermore, the projected learning procedure adjusts the positions of the prototype in order to minimize the objective function as well. Selecting prototypes mitigates the risk of overfitting while safe guarding the notion of locality. The experimental results after performing number of various evaluations clearly demonstrates that LMDL significantly increases the predictive performance over the other related existing methods. The experimental results stated that the proposed LMDL achieved nearly 82% in E-coli dataset, 94% in Breast Cancer Dataset and 98% in Iris Dataset for all metrics such as accuracy, precision, recall, and F-Measure.

Table of Contents

List of Figures

List of Tables

Abbreviations

ACNN	-	Adaptive Condensed Nearest Neighbor
ANN	-	Artificial Neural Network
ASVM	-	Asymmetric Support Vector Machine
AUC	-	Area Under-Cover
CIL	-	Class Imbalance Learning
CM-KLOGR	-	Confusion Matrix- based Kernel LOGistic Regression
CSL	-	Cost-Sensitive Learning
DEC	-	Diversified Ensemble Classifiers
DM	-	Data Mining
FKNN	-	Fuzzy K Nearest Neighbor
FN	-	False Negative
FP	-	False Positive
GA	-	Genetic Algorithm
GFRNN	-	Gravitational Fixed Radius Neural Network
GPD	-	Generalized Probabilistic Descent
HM	-	Harmonic Mean
IR	-	Imbalance Ratio
KDD	-	Knowledge Discovery Database
KNN	-	K-Nearest Neighbor
LMDL	-	Local Mahalanobis Distance Learning
MLA	-	Machine Learning Algorithm
MCE	-	Minimum Classification Error
MLP	-	Multi-Layer Perceptron
NN	-	Neural Network
NPV	-	Negative Predictive Value
OAA	-	One-Against-All
OAA-DB	-	One-Against-All with Data Balancing
OSS	-	One Sided Selection
PC	-	Principal Component Analysis
PG	-	Prototype Generation
PPV	-	Positive Predictive Value
PS	-	Prototype Selection
RF	-	Random Forest

RNN	-	Recurrent Neural Network
SCG	-	Scaled Conjugate Gradient
SMOTE	-	Synthetic Minority Oversampling Technique
SNN	-	Structure Nearest Neighbor
SVM	-	Support Vector Machine
TN	-	True Negative
TP	-	True Positive
UCI	-	University of California Irvine

Chapter 1 Introduction

Recently, data is accumulating tremendously in almost all fields such as scientific research, industrial organizations, educational institutions, business sectors, medical science, government organizations, etc. The relationships between data, valid patterns and unknown data are discovered from vast amount of data warehouses, databases or other repositories by using data analysis tools in DM process. There are five analysis categories in DM tasks such as dependency analysis, classification, data summarization, prediction and segmentation. Among the five categories, classification is considered as one of the most important task in DM, which is used in many fields such as decision theory, NN, statistics, MLA, pattern recognition and so on. In classification tasks, supervised learning methods are used, where new objects are assigned from a set of classes according to the attribute value of the objects. This research thesis focuses on uncertain data classification with respect to different data for example, medical or normal data. Subsequently, the imbalance information issue has attracted much consideration of the legitimate MLA, DM. The two levels of algorithms such as data and algorithmic levels consists more number of imbalance information, and the most important characteristic is the distribution of skewed class. The further section describes the detailed steps of the uncertain DM process.

Overview of Data Mining

The techniques are integrated to extract/mining the vast uncertain information from various disciplines namely data visualization, temporal data analysis, database and data warehouse technology, information retrieval. A valuable information are searched, viewed and browsed from different angles by using DM techniques, which is also known as knowledge extraction, data archaeology and pattern analysis. Knowledge Discovery in Databases (KDD) is a popular term used to represent the DM process, where relations and patterns are identified from large-scale database. The statistical method used in DM process is considered as one of the successful process to retrieve the useful information from raw data.

Generally, useful knowledge and information are mined sequentially by processing the more number of uncertain data. In DM process, the text files or other different kinds of data are considered as special categories of data sources, which is an interdisciplinary research field. The uncertain DM process is shown in Figure 1.1 and explained below. There are several steps includes cleaning, integration, transformation, selection, etc for DM process (i.e., iterative process) which are explained as below.

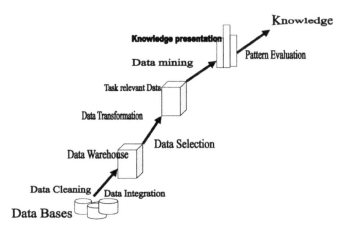

Figure 1.1: Detailed Uncertain Data Mining Steps

- **Step 1: Cleaning**: The source file data in real-world are corrupted, incomplete and inconsistent, where the redundant and missing data are handled by cleaning task. In this process, the deficient data and exceptions are identified by different techniques, and also used to smooth the inaccurate values, filled or removed the lost values.

- **Step 2: Integration:** The information is collected from various sources data which contains dissimilar data definitions in integration process. In this process, a single coherent data store is used to insert a data rather than using the multiple data sources.

- **Step 3: Selection:** In DM process, the relevant data are extracted from source data is known as data selection process.

- **Step 4: Transformation:** This process plays an important role in DM task, because the source data are arranged into proper format by using data management functions such as attributes construction, normalization, aggregations and smoothing.

- **Step 5: Mining:** In this process, smart methods are used for extracting the data patterns.

- **Step 6: Pattern Evaluation:** From the extracted pattern set, interested patterns of users are determined in this mission.

- **Step 7: Knowledge Presentation:** The knowledge of DM is visualized to end user, where it has a variety of application area as well as banking, biology, e-commerce etc.

History of Data Uncertainty

A data consists of noises is also known as uncertain data which is different from unique or correct values of data. The characteristic of huge uncertain data is defined as data veracity or uncertainty. Nowadays, sensor networks within enterprises contain plenty of uncertain data in both structured and unstructured format, because data grows in different scales like variety, velocity, volume and uncertainty (1/veracity). According to real-world data and analyses, a various kinds of uncertainty should be studied which is present in vast amount of data to make a confident business decisions. The quality of underlying results is improved by ignoring the uncertainty in core data, because it is considered as one of the main problems in DM. From the DM survey for uncertainty problem, classification is one of the most studied techniques to solve these problems. Classification uncertainty can be predictable as posterior probabilities by non-parametric classifiers at the per-case basis (pixels or objects). Additionally, existing supervised classification techniques provides poor results, because the learning dataset consists of incorrect labels. But, the traditional techniques assume that the labels in leaning samples are true due to estimation of parameters from noise labels. Therefore, uncertainty of data occurs which leads to data loss, incomplete data and delay transmission.

Significant Source of Data Uncertainty

The deterministic data streams are extracted in less complication, when compared with task of mining on uncertain data streams. This reason behind this is that the uncertain data are expanding exponentially than deterministic data. A useful information system is built by representing the uncertainty in an effective way, because it plays a vital and positive role in DM. In general, uncertain data sources are classified into the following categories:

- ❖ **Incompleteness:** In most of the dataset, some values are absent or missed (lack of relevant information).
- ❖ **Imprecision:** A values cannot be measured with suitable precision from the existence of data, which will leads to imprecision.
- ❖ **Imperfect:** Due to lack of information or subjective error on part of some observer, imperfection may arise.
- ❖ **Randomness:** A data series/events are lacked in specific direction, which leads to improper explanation or prediction in a statistical or probabilistic manner. Then these data are considered as random data.
- ❖ **Vagueness:** This is a subcategory of imprecision (fuzzy valued imprecision).
- ❖ **Inconsistence:** A single variable contains too many conflicting values which have led to this situation. i.e., The DM process can extract too many information from many sources.
- ❖ **Ignorance:**Due to lack of relative certainty knowledge for number of statements, a data sources can be ignored.

DM incorporating uncertainty is important, because it puts the study of DM in a more realistic setting. Equally important is what the role of uncertainty possible to play. Different approaches have been developed to deal with different types of uncertainty.

Significant Challenges for Uncertain Data Techniques

The previous unknown knowledge of uncertain data is discovered from real-world dataset by using DM techniques, which is an active research area because of its practical applications and theoretical challenges. According to uncertain data, the DM faces these following main challenges are described as:

- ❖ **Dimensionality Constraint:** The data is collected by man and machines over a period of time during the course of on-going patient treatment. A raw data consists of redundant and irrelevant information which leads to high-dimensionality of data. Before, extracting the information from raw data, it should be pre-processed and reduce the dimensionality by using appropriate effective feature selection techniques.

- ❖ **Class Imbalance:** A one target class is formed by having a majority of data instances, which is known as class imbalance problem and most of the medical data are affected by this problem. The distribution in target class is balanced by using suitable over-sampling and under-sampling techniques.

- ❖ **Missing/Incomplete data:** This is a common problem associated with human and machine reading errors occurred during the monitoring of the patient. There is subtle need for effective imputation methods to fill the missing gaps.

- ❖ **Heterogeneous Data:** Heterogeneity in medical data is one of the important performance bottlenecks. A various types of heterogeneous data are obtained from medical dataset includes nominal, continuous, interval scaled and categorical data. To deal with this type of heterogeneity data, effective pre-processing techniques should be used.

- ❖ **Uncertainty/Ambiguity:** The presence of uncertain and ambiguous data measurements is an inherent part of captured data. It is also a common problem associated with human and machine reading errors occurred during patient health monitoring. It necessitates fuzziness in decision-making models.

Taxonomy of Uncertainty Data Mining

The companies aimed to concentrate on most important information by using DM, which is used to extract the hidden predictive information from the large data warehouse. The behaviors of hidden patterns are predicted by DM tools for helping the business people to make a knowledge-driven and pro-active decision. The DM tools are handled the certain data as well as uncertain data. The source of outdated data, missing data, errors and inaccuracy in measurement are often associated with uncertainty data problems, which leads to poor performance in existing techniques. The taxonomy of uncertain DM is shown in the Figure: 1.2.

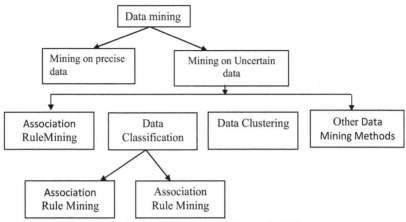
Figure 1.2: Hierarchal Structure of Uncertain DM

In DM process, the data are analyzed and extracted from huge dataset by employing one or more learning techniques for gaining the knowledge in the form of generalization or model of data. There are several techniques used in uncertain DM process includes data clustering, classification, association rule mining and so on. According to attribute values, a class obtains a new object in a given set of classes which is the considered as major objective of uncertain data classification. A training set consists of known class labels with all associated objects which is used by classification approach to build a model for classifying the new objects. These uncertain DM techniques are briefly described in the following section.

Association Rule Mining

The reliable and useful results are obtained by preserving the authentication rules and eliminate the harmful spurious rules in association rule mining. The spurious rules are prevented by calculating statistical association rules, but true rules are lost severely due to the presence of data errors. The authentic rules are used to avoid the spurious rules by making a clear decision and the balance between these rules are discovered by reliability, which is a key value of association rule mining. In high-dimensional data, these conventional algorithms discovernumerous false spurious rules due to available of large number of potential rules. The spurious rules problems is considered as a critical barrier due to more number of rules generated in vast dataset and rule mining algorithms for achieving high reliability. Also, the error and imprecision is considered as a major source problem for reliability issues in uncertainty data. In every stage of rule mining, the quantitative process are misled by errors raised from source data, which will automatically leads to generate the spurious rules and authenticate rules loss. Therefore, in order to avoid the uncertainty of data or spurious rules, intensive association rule mining should be studied[1].

Data Clustering

In data management, the most important challenging task is to cluster the uncertain data streams due to time and space requirements for processing the tuples at high speed. The degree of similarity among objects are calculated by using salient features of data for automatic classification is considered as the fundamental concepts of clustering and also recognized as most important research field in DM. Calculating the similarity between documents is a vital step in almost all document clustering algorithms. Usually, in feature space, the number of dimension is directly proportional to the computation cost, so the computation efficiency can be enhanced by minimizing the feature space. Recently, feature selection for document categorization has become an attractive area of research.

Data Classification

The classification models are constructed from the input of given dataset by assigning an object to particular class according to its similarity with other objects. In classification, finding the probability of objects belongs to class or the closeness of objects with other samples of that class resembles the degree of certainty. The uncertain data classification is defined as the various classes are fully/partly overlapped, which leads to poor classification results (i.e., hard to classify the data into particular class) because of less attributes information. Therefore, the characterization of imprecision and uncertainty are failed while using probability theory framework [2]. The classification technique is classified into two types such as (i) Supervised technique and (ii) Unsupervised technique. A classifier is built to implement the supervised methods, where manually labeled samples are used to train the classifiers, but, training datasets which are collected by MLA algorithms are used also for training the classifiers. The common supervised techniques are K-Nearest Neighbor (K-NN) classifiers, Support Vector Machine (SVM), logistic regression, Naive Bayes (NB) classifier etc. The most widely applicable is unsupervised techniques, which does not require any training data. The anomaly scenarios and all devices datasets are combined and their data are labeled. The cross validation process is carried out by selecting the training and testing dataset, where combined training dataset are constructed by unsupervised learning technique.

Essential Uncertain Data Classification Techniques

A model can be built from given input dataset is known as classification technique which is also named as an organized approach. The class label and attribute set relationship are found out by employing a learning algorithm of each technique for the given input data.

Decision Tree

In uncertainty data, prediction and classification are carried out by powerful tool is known as decision tree which consists of nodes of root, leaves and branches. A set of attributes describes the sequential classification process which is expressed by simple recursive structure (i.e., decision tree). A test on an attribute and outcome of these test and class labels are represented by each internal node, branch and leaf in tree [3]. The root node of the tree is known as the starting node in the tree. The properties of decision tree are described as below:

- The name of class is labeled to each leaf. The attributes names are labeled to root and each internal node, which is known as decision node.

- The node's attribute or disjoint values are labeled to the branches and each internal node contains a set of minimum two children nodes. The legal values are formed from the labels on the arcs which lefts from a parent node for attribute of parent.

The classification process of decision tree starts with the root of the tree and ends with the leaf node. The outcome for the test is determined at each decision node and shifts the results to the root of sub-tree. The label class of the case is determined, when this process reaches the leaf node of the tree.

Neural Network

NN are the other method developed to eliminate various pattern classification problems present in uncertain data classification. The different layers of network set contains neurons which are joined together with many links and the weights (i.e., estimated values) are presented in these links to store the facial features information. There are three layers presents in the NN such as input, hidden and output layers, where the necessary information are fed into the network in input layer. The challenging problems are resolved, data are processed and the network is trained in the second layer, which is made up of one or two hidden layers [4]. The output of the network is provided in the last layer of NN, which is used to compare the results with comparator by using pre-defined target values. A feed-forward network and Recurrent Neural Network (RNN) are the two different topologies present in NN. The signals of feed-forward network are travel in a single direction, which consists of three layers namely, input, hidden and output layers. Because of the single direction, feed-forward network is considered as a non-recurrent network. The general architecture of NN is shown in the Figure: 1.3

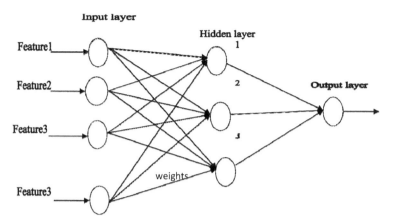

Figure 1.3: Structure of Neural Network

Initially, the calculations are predicted in the processing element layers by allowing the input data into those layers. The element from each processing system provides an evaluation on the basis of weighted sum present in the inputs. The calculated values are feed into next layer as new input and this process continues until it reaches the each and every layers of NN for obtaining the output. The threshold transfer function helps in quantifying the output neuron from output layer. The records are given to the network only once in a time, but the input values' weights are adjusted every time, which are strategic features of NN. Until all cases are presented to the network, this process will continues. The correct class labels are predicted for given input samples by adjusting the weights of the network and trained by itself during learning phase. The NN has an ability to classify the patterns that are not trained in learning phase as well classify the noisy data with high tolerance.

Rule Based Classifiers

The high-level if-then classification rules are easy to interpret with rule based classifiers, where the rules are classified into two parts namely, consequent and antecedent rules. A predictor attribute values are referred by set of conditions that is specified by rule antecedent (i.e., if part), where the rule predicts the class for any example which satisfies the condition in if part is defined as rule consequent (i.e., then part). The most important algorithms namely sequential covering rule induction and decision tree induction are used to generate these rules [5].

Support Vector Machine

In statistical learning, SVM is considered as root for classification technique and used in many applications such as text categorization and recognition of handwritten digit. The curse of dimensionality is avoided by using SVM with high dimensional data. The five-fold cross validation is calculated with SVM, but it does not provide the probability estimation directly.

K-Nearest Neighbor

In learning algorithm, KNN classifier is considered as non-parametric lazy algorithm, where data samples are classified according to the selected number of KNN. The some assumptions used in KNN are described as below:

- KNN has the concept of distance, because it assumes that the data is in feature space. Therefore, the distance between vectors is computed by Euclidean distance.
- A class label and set of vectors are associated with every training vector.
- The classification is influenced by neighbors decided by K.

The KNN mostly used the majority rule, where the individual class value counts are calculated by the classification of nearest neighbors from all KNN [6-7]. The duplicate counts are avoided by the odd number of K, where the samples are classified by using majority count with class value.

Problem Statement of the Research Work

The imbalance class distribution may happen regularly with learning in many applications. In real-world dataset, the distribution of imbalance class occurs when minority/positive class is represented insufficiently. The significant problem statements are addressed below.

- The Classification is performed in different datasets but major problem is unstructured class. When the class has less number of samples is called as minority class, whereas majority has more number of samples is considered as unstructured dataset. This problem will affect the performance of data classification techniques.
- The imbalance data are small in size and high dimensionality especially on the minority class. The features lack of the discriminate ability and further lead to the poor performance in classification.
- The informational indexes with imbalance class makes an additional challenge for KNN characterization rule, because there is no identical number of representatives for each class, which makes a difficulty to determine the value k. The class imbalance problems are handled by presenting a class-explicit global weighting method.
- In uncertain data classification, the numerous datasets are used, which include noisy and incomplete data for example, missing of data row or column. These dataare degrading the classification efficiency.

Scope and Significant Contribution

Imbalance in data classification is a frequently discussed problem that is not well achieved by classical classification techniques. In minority class, the problem of learning the binary and multiple-classification model for large dataset is tackled by implementing the proposed algorithms with higher accuracy constraint. The contribution and scope of this research work is explained in this section as follows:

- The data-point-specific k is chosen by developing an effective ACNN technique for finding the each training data points and CNN is used to classify the value of k accurately.

- The local information about neighborhood data points are calculated by estimating a suitable k value using ACNN for each query point. A non-linear regression problem are developed due to the value of k, and this problem are avoided by using feed forward Multi-Layer Perceptron (MLP) with Scaled Conjugate Gradient (SCG) learning algorithm for calculating the k-terrain.

- Developing the kernelized version of the proposed method based on the concept of Kernel Trick makes it highly flexible and more efficient.

- The performance of nearest neighbor classifier is enhanced by developing a Local Mahalanobis Distance Learning (LMDL). A multiple distance metrics are learned and also considers the influence of neighborhood for reduced set of input samples in LMDL.

Thesis Organization

This section explains the organization of the research work which consists of five major chapters and the brief discussion of current chapters are explained below.

Chapter 1 introduces the Knowledge Discovery Process and the uncertain DM concepts. It discusses the source, major techniques of uncertain data. Moreover, the scope and contribution of this research work are described with problem statement of the traditional imbalance classification techniques.

Chapter 2 presents a survey of the existing uncertain data handling techniques, and traditional uncertain data as well as imbalanced data classification methods in DM. Also discusses the advantages and issues in the existing techniques to be addressed.

Chapter 3 describes the imbalanced data classification using A-CNN method. The issues of binary- and multi-class imbalance data classification are resolvedby using this proposed method. The experimental analysis is conducted on different medical datasets also, compared the existing and proposed method performance.

Chapter 4 describes the performance of nearest neighbor classifier which is enhanced by an efficient distance metric namely LMDL. The multiple distance metrics are learned and also considers the influence of neighborhood for less number of input samples by proposed method. Moreover, experimental analyses of proposed and existing techniques performances are discussed.

Chapter 5 describes the summary of this research work with future work.

Chapter 2: Literature Survey

The importance of classification plays a crucial role in DM and MLA community works. Many organizations used ever-growing volumes of operational data used for DM techniques enormously thereafter to predict and describe expressive relationship between objects. To develop better classifier that performs imbalanced dataset, usually called as Class Imbalance Learning (CIL) methods. CIL method is generally categorized as Internal and External methods. The pre-processing of the training datasets included External method to balance datasets and whereas, the modifications of learning algorithms used internal methods to deduct sensitiveness and imbalance. The main advantage of external methods is their independent of underlying classifier. This research work has conducted an elaborated literature survey on internal, external and hybrid methods. The data is said to be imbalanced whenever a class in a classification task is under lower prior probability (i.e., under represented).

The major problem that arises is due to increase in number of patterns rule the classifier decision boundaries are at the expense of minority classes that are expressed by large number of patterns rule that are represented by small number of patterns. The majority and minority classes are classified into high and low class accuracies which do not redirect on critical situations during classification. Thereby examining the problems occurred due to the data produced by standard algorithm by MLA without regulating the outcome threshold value may be major mistake. The generation of a high number of false-negative predictions decreases the model performance in improper dataset. The spot light of this survey is to know skewness towards minority class (positive) generally causes the generation of a high number of false-negative predictions, which lower the model's performance on the positive class compared to the performance on the negative (majority) class. A survey has been conducted for this research work to show the various classification techniques, their advantages and disadvantages towards improving the performance in imbalanced data set. The spotlight of this survey is to understand the broad contours that affect classification performance in majority and minority classes. The study of various existing classification techniques supports us to better appreciate the challenges possessed by Imbalance data set. The study of these emerging techniques lead to understand the performance lack based on certain parameters such as accuracy, recall, precision, F-mean and G-mean.

Survey on Imbalanced Learning Methods

Imbalanced dataset problem is a classification problem where class priors are highly unequal and imbalanced. Due to the immense growth in science and technology huge amount of unprocessed data in the MLA is generated. Each dataset possesses its own information structure and distribution. In some datasets imbalanced determination is provided due to the biased distribution of classes. That is, when managing imbalanced information sets, classifiers should have to consider minor examples as major examples. The imbalanced learning problem is unequal distribution of data between the classes where one class contains more samples compared to another class. Due to irregularity learning issues, it turns out to be hard for the classifier to learn the minority class samples. Without accounting for imbalanced prior, a classifier may adapt to predict always the class with majority. The cost of misclassifying class points that have high value, a classifier that forecasts class with majority is not suitable. To handle imbalance problems methods have been developed and studied. A solution to the above problem is to sample again in the training set. Re-sampling helps to change the training set priors by either increasing points in minority class or by decreasing points in majority class. Another technique of dealing with class imbalance includes an appropriate feature selection, one-class learners, and cost-sensitive learners which explicitly take misclassification cost into account when learning.

To deal with imbalanced learning problem critical work has been performed, which can be sorted into four classes: sampling based technique, cost based technique, Kernel based techniques, and active learning techniques.

Sampling Based Techniques

Sampling methods with distinct properties such as under-sampling, focused and random oversampling fell into section. The majority-class as per the given examples are randomly removed unless a specific class ratio is encountered according to random under-sampling. The minority-class as per the examples are removed randomly unless those are randomly duplicated to reach specific class ratio is reached. Novel synthetic examples are generated in the neighboring existing minority-class examples other than duplicating them directly. An oversampling method called, Synthetic minority oversampling technique (SMOTE) generated synthetic examples that are generated in the neighboring existing class of minority not specifically duplicating them directly.

The fundamental knowledge of understanding the analysis and discovery from raw data to process support decision making. The continuous extension of the available data in many large-scale, network systems etc., are complex systems in the security, surveillance, finance and Internet that becomes difficult to advance the basic knowledge discovery understanding and raw data analysis to support decision-making process. Even though the data engineering techniques have discovered real-time applications and succeeded, the difficulty of examining data imbalance is moderately a new challenge that has attained attention from industries of academia. The presentation of algorithms examined in existence of non-represented data and performs class distribution of skews.

The data set of imbalanced data constitutes complex characteristics which needs new principles, understandings, algorithms, and methods to transmit huge amount of raw data effectively into knowledge and representation of information. The imbalanced learning difficulties has received a particularly compromised the performance of all most standard algorithms of learning. The imbalanced learning problem has extracted the imbalanced data that automatically settles the performance of most standard algorithms. Moreover, the standard algorithm, assume or expect class distribution of data with balance data to compromise performance of standard learning algorithms. Balanced class distributions or misclassification of equal costs are assumed to most standard algorithms. Therefore, datasets with imbalanced data sets fail to express properly data with distributive characteristics of the and effectively provided accuracies having unfavorable with classes of the data.Haibo He, and Edwardo A. Garcia, [8] developed, an under-sampling methods that deduced the samples with from majority class to equalize majority and minority classes. Random under-sampling was performed some important contexts may be left out from the majority class which was a major constraint. Moreover, this method proposed in the cost-based sampling technique, during the sample generation process, consideration of minority samples was not needed as overlapping problem could occur. The distribution of samples of minority used the weighted distribution. Depending upon the importance of minority samples weight is assigned to minority sample. The difficulty to classify samples got higher weight than other. Samples which were difficult to classify got higher weight than others. More samples were generated for the sample having a higher weight.

Inderjeet Mani, and I. Zhang, [9] developed a K-NN based approach and used to handle the imbalance data distribution issue and to achieve under sampling. The four approaches like, NearMiss-1, NearMiss-2, NearMiss-3 and most distant method were used. For under sampling, the average distances of the major samples with three minority samples that were closer and smallest were selected in NearMiss-1 method. The samples from majority section that were very close to all minority samples and selection of samples that were based on average distances of three farthest samples with minority samples in NearMiss-2 method. Each minority samples that were surrounded by majority samples were guaranteed in NearMiss3 method. The number of closest majority samples is nominated for each minority sample. The majority samples with distant methods achieved majority samples because of average distances are close to three minority samples which are selected for under-sampling.

The unbalanced data set is required for classification research in a new study hotspot in MLA field and attained theoretical and practical values for exact MLA systems and also forwarding studies with new machine study ideas. The applicative fields with unbalanced data set exist in current fields like, for credit cards that were processed by frauds, information retrieval, medical diagnosis, classification of document, etc. The rate of recognizing minority class is very important.

Theunbalanced dataset by price with wrong division pays a larger price when majority classes are wrongly classified by minority class.The majority class and low recognition rate of minority class tends to perform traditional classification methods. In the field of pattern recognition and MLA, researchers concentrate more attention to the minority class samples so as to improve the performance which acts as an important space to improvise. Yang Yong, [10] developed genetic algorithm and k-means Clustering algorithm. The developed method performed two stages, the first stage k-means clustering is used to determine clusters among minority set and the genetic algorithm played in second stage, is utilized to determine the resampling sets in minority samples. The University of California Irvine (UCI) standard data sets were simulated based on training samples. During the classification, results showed improvised accuracy for KNN classifier that utilized scattered training set with newly balanced dataset. The burden of classification phase did not increase algorithm that finished in disposing of training dataset. The problem of handling class imbalance learning was efficiently used to ensemble the techniques.

The traditional MLA disappointed to accomplish better results because of distributed skew class. The performance of facing imbalanced datasets in SVM, extensively researched to show remarkable success in many application area ranging from image retrieval to classification. The SVM properties failed in balancing imbalanced datasets when positive instances resulted in negative number of instances. The modification in the algorithm tried to improve efficient SVM on imbalanced dataset by modifying the algorithms. The pretreatment of sampling datasets by modifying the algorithm itself was difficult such that the efficient SVM decreased outnumber with positive instances. Due to the selection of typical samples, the combinational optimization was complex. S. Zou, et al., [11] developed a new sampling approach that was based on Genetic Algorithm to balance again in the imbalanced training dataset for SVM. The coded samples were represented as binary string that represented as selected or not. The performance of SVM classifiers evaluated the fitness function in Genetic Algorithm that employed Area Under ROC Curve (AUC). The protein domain boundary was implemented when the method faced imbalanced problem. The developed method obtained 70% prediction accuracy with 0.905 of AUC value. The experimental results showed that this method was prior to individual SVM and better than random sampling for the imbalanced training dataset.

Cost-Based Techniques

The learning algorithms used both data and modified data. The classification was performed for higher misclassification cost that was assigned to overall learning cost. The costs were specified in the form of cost matrices. The main drawbacks that were produced from the developed method were cost-sensitive towards methods, since lack of knowledge on how the actual values are determined. The most cases are neither known from the data nor by any expert.

The classifiers usually try to decrease the number of errors usually in MLA. The setting costs of different settings have valid errors. Appropriately, the costs of different errors are unequal for many real-world applications. The MLA and DM communities are in fact, cost-sensitive. From past years, the learning methods have attained Cost Sensitive Learning (CSL) methods. Even though there were much efforts on research that devoted for making decision trees that were cost effective and only a few networks discuss about cost-sensitive neural networks, which is not possible to achieve cost-sensitive decision tree learning methods that are directly fed to neural networks. The imbalance problem in the class is recognized as a critical problem in DM and MLA such a problem came across a large number of domains and in some cases caused negative effect seriously on MLA performance. J. Xiao, et al., [12] developed a CSL that is a dynamic classifier ensembles technique with CSL. The output of ensemble classifiers combined a new cost sensitive measure that improved the performance. For handling imbalance handling class learning that analyzed the comparative of external and internal methods to perform imbalance in handling class was performed. The data overlapping and data shifting deeply study about the ensemble classifiers. For handling class imbalance learning a comparative study of internal and external methods for usage of learning imbalance in class was performed. The results revealed about properties of intrinsic of data overlapping and data shifting. Z. H. Zhou, and Xu-Ying Liu, [13] developed soft-ensemble (soft voting) and hard-ensemble (hard voting) two novel methods using threshold moving concept. The output threshold for inexpensive classes moved the output threshold towards the inexpensive classes so that it was easy to misclassify the examples that attained higher cost and was difficult to misclassify. The limitation of dynamic classifier ensemble method is ensemble technique with CSL. To combine the generated output of ensemble classifier, a new cost sensitive measure was developed. Both external and internal methods were considered for comparative analysis was conducted. The properties of proposed data shifting and data overlapping intrinsic properties were studied deeply accordingly to the analysis.

The basic issue to be resolved is that they tend to ignore or over fit the minority class. Hence, research efforts have been made on the development of a good learning model which can predict rare cases more accurately to lower the total risk. In recent years, approaches with ensemble properties have become a popular way of classifying imbalanced data, because emphasizing the minority class regions by rebalancing the training subset from the data level or by applying different costs from the algorithm level was easily adapted. Also, the idea of combining multiple classifiers itself can bring down the probability of overfitting to a great extent. Particular techniques like under sampling and oversampling usually used with ensembles to increase generalization of forecasting the class of minority. Shuo Wang, and Xin Yao, [14] developed an extension of SVM known as Asymmetric SVM (ASVM) for false predictions and reducing cost from classes of distinct. The major aim of the developed ASVM was to permit false-positive rate and user tolerance as specified by the user. One of the strength of ASVM is that it can increase the accuracy of the overall model with improved training time. Y. S. Ihn, et al., [15] have proposed a staged framework for preprocessing data to support DM. The proposed framework pushes the data imbalance and cost sensitivity and of customer retention data into the data preprocessing itself. One of the strength of the framework is the applicability in the field of customer churning or attrition for the industries.

Ensemble Level Approaches

The performance of the overall system is improved by Ensemble methods. The efficiency of Ensemble methods is highly reliable and free from the error committed by the base learner. The performance of ensemble methods strongly depends on accuracy and diversity of base learner. The simplest method to produce diverse base classifier is by influencing the training data. The methods include for ensemble level approaches are kernel-based methods and kernel classifier identification.

The task of finding rare events or objects is usually formulated as a supervised learning problem. Training instances are collected for both target and no target events and, then, a classifier is trained on the collected data to predict future instances. Researchers in the community of DM that has been used SVMs for learning algorithm due to the strong theoretical foundation in SVMs with strong foundations with theoretical and excellence in empirical successes in distinct patterns like image retrieval, text classification, and hand-writing recognition. However, detection of rare-object and event mining during other training instances significantly outnumbered the instances of training that can be skewed severely toward target class. Therefore, the results showed a False-Negative Rate that has highly excessive identifying important objects with target (e.g., a surveillance event or a disease-causing agent) and can result in catastrophic consequences. Gang Wu, and Edward Y. Chang, [16] proposed a kernel-boundary-alignment algorithm for handling class distribution imbalance problem with the help of SVM. Using a simple example, the method showed that SVMs was impacted from false negatives of high incidences when the instances of training and classes of target were heavily numbered from instances of training of a non-target class. Accordingly, the method was adjusted to the class boundary at the time of modifying the kernel matrix, according to the data imbalance distribution. From the analysis of theory as per the empirical study, the experimental results showed that kernel boundary-alignment algorithm worked on datasets effectively. The proposed model improved on prediction accuracy of SVMs which was sensitivity to class boundaries.

ZhiQiang Zeng, and ShunZhi Zhu, [17] proposed a new oversampling strategy based on kernel function has been proposed to train SVM. The method first preprocessed the data using both out-class and in-class that generates instances with minority feature space, then the images with pre-stage of synthetic samples were determined based on relation between distance of feature space and input space. At last, these images at pre-stage were appended to original class with minority data set in order to train SVM. The real data sets were compared and indicated with existing methods of over-sampling technique, the samples generated by the proposed strategy have the higher quality. Therefore, from results, the classification of SVM have effectively sampled both in-class and out-class sampling to generate minority instances in the feature space, then the pre-images of the synthetic samples were found based on a distance relation between input space and feature space. Finally, these pre-images were appended to the original minority class data set to train a SVM. The experiments on real data sets indicated that compared with existing over-sampling technique, the samples generated by the proposed strategy have the higher quality. From results, the effectiveness of classification by SVM with imbalanced data sets was improved.

Active Learning Based Methods

In semi-supervised learning labeled and unlabeled samples are available. It will be highly expensive to label the samples manually and also, to improve the classification accuracy, active learning methods focus on acquiring labels for those unlabeled data samples.The active learner chooses the unlabeled samples which are closer to decision boundary and most uncertain. In the traditional approach, the human annotator (oracle) exists which gives labels to unlabeled samples when the learner raise queries for labels. There are three main categories of this traditional approach such as pool based active learning, stream based active learning and query construction based active learning in domains of valuable where non available data were readily available, but training labels obtained are expensive. Active learning is an essential task in classifying in MLA as well as DM, as it may hold the data scarcity problem for solving key problems like lack of labeled data

Traditional supervised learning algorithms use whatever labeled data is provided to induce a model. Asan active learning results a learner degree controls by allowing selecting instances that are added and labeled among the training dataset. An active learner starts with label set with small features selects one or more informative instances of query from a huge unnamed pool, these labeled queries and recurs. The learner achieves to acquire accuracy with high rate as labeling effort with little is possible. Attaining training labels is costly so therefore, an active learning unlabeled data available readily that is valuable in domains. Active learning is important in DM and MLA for classification as it solved the data scarcity problems, which is an effective process. Webpage classification like image, movie, news articles, face classification is important to have correctly labeled sets with examples of supervised learning, even though the labels are given by experts and thus acquires time consumption and costly. Although, previous work with active learning is "pool-based" of unlabeled examples and also select the examples for raising the queries among the pool and label them.

Charles X. Ling, and Jun Du, [18] proposed novel Active learners with Direct Query construction (called ADQ for short) and labels for their query. This was also called "membership query" studied in theoretical setting but mostly previously. More specifically, the method first studied a definite active learner for decision tree algorithm (called Tree-ADQ) to examine queries. Then a general active learner is proposed which has worked based on any learning algorithm (called wrapper ADQ, as it was like a wrapper enclosing any base learning algorithm). The experiments showed that ADQ algorithms constructed queries that reduced the predictive error rates more quickly compared to the traditional pool-based algorithms. The ADQ algorithm was also more computationally efficient. Furthermore, ADQ was also easily adapted to work with a given pool of unlabeled examples. The ADQ algorithms were also shown to be more time-efficient than the traditional pool-based methods. Burr Settles, and Mark Craven, [19] have presented a detailed analysis of active learning for sequence labeling tasks. In particular, this paper has described and criticized the query selection strategies used with probabilistic sequence models to date, and proposed several novel strategies to address some of their shortcomings. The large-scale empirical evaluation demonstrated that the proposed methods performed well when compared with the state of the art in active learning with sequence models. These methods included information density, sequence vote entropy, and Fisher information.

Survey on Review of Multi-Class Classification for Imbalanced Data

Classification in Multiclass is a critical difficulty task in MLA. In multiclass classification for each instance in the learning set is a part of number of set of predefined labels. The correct voting and prediction stands as a critical task in the imbalance data multiclass classification scenario. Performance and Accuracy of multiclass classification be influenced by prediction and voting of new class data. When new class of imbalanced data is assigned it generates confusion and thereby degrades the performance and decreases the accuracy of classifier.

The problem of classification has been inspected for many years. Based on this problem, the binary classification can be categorized into two main categories of problems, which are binary classification and multi-class classification. Generally, classification problem in multi-class is much dangerous to handle binary classification problem. The number of classes increased the complexity in learning inductive algorithm. The domains created more complex problems like problem occurred during classification of imbalanced multi-class data that handled such difficulty. The research examinations presented researches did not enhance the performance using binary classification techniques, which solved the problem due to imbalanced data in classification of multi class. The techniques for balancing the data as per the minority class is enriched, the accuracy in majority class gets tendency to lower. At last, due to high ratio during the comparison of majority class minority class, the total accuracy reduces. PiyasakJeatrakul, and KokWai Wong, [20] demonstrated about imbalanced data using multi-class One-Against-All with Data Balancing (OAA-DB) algorithm that solved the imbalanced problem. One-Against-All (OAA) approach combined data balancing technique that was applied to multi-binary classification technique. The integration of under sampling using Complementary Neural Network (CMTNN) and the over -sampling technique using SMOTE were sampled. Three multi-class datasets from the UCI machine learning repository that balanced Glass Identification data, Scale data, and Yeast data. The experiment was conducted using three multi-class sets of data that were obtained using three multi-class datasets from the UCI machine learning repository that identifies data, Yeast data, and Balance Scale data. The results obtained after classification were compared using macro F1 and accuracy. The obtained results from OAA-DB algorithm indicated and enhanced classification performance for imbalanced multi data. The results obtained from OAA-DB algorithm improved the classification performance via OAA-DB algorithm for the multi-class imbalanced data, and performed better other than techniques in each test case. The classification and performance of maintained minority classes maintained the total accuracy in terms of overall performance.

PiyasakJeatrakul, et al., [21] developed a performance algorithm when there was data imbalance that combined training data among uneven majority classes. Three types of MLA for the classification of test sets included were Artificial Neural Network (ANN), SVM, and k-NN. The performance of the results was accepted and evaluated for comparing in terms of performance that is widely accepted measures for imbalance problem which were AUC and G-mean. The obtained results indicated the combined technique by CMTNN and SMOTE that performed well than other techniques in almost all test cases. The difficult part is the minority classes needed to be completely recognized. The pattern classification including speech recognition, text document classification, object recognition etc.,

Applications comes under Multi-class pattern classification that includes object recognition, speech recognition, text document classification, etc., Using NN multi-class pattern classification two-class NN which cannot be a trivial extension. GuobinOu, and Yi Lu Murphey, [22] developed an application related to multiclass pattern classification with the help of neural networks. A competitive study of mutli-class neural learning focused on difficulties occurring in neural network. A deep study on K-class pattern classification was explained using neural networks in their work.

Distinct architectures of two networks were designed namely single neural network systems and multiple neural networks. Three distinct modeling approaches such as OAA, OAO, and etc., were adapted.

Survey on Review of Nearest Neighbor Based Method on Imbalanced Dataset

In the real world, the imbalanced learning data that involved financial fraud determination medical diagnosis, network intrusion detection, Bioinformatics etc., were almost in static cases but some of the cases are dynamic because the samples increased continuously. So the sequential imbalance data methods with classifications are presented. The results obtained in the earlier research exposed that the traditional methods undergone classification approaches are exposed when datasets are dealing with imbalance datasets. The KNN algorithm with classic characteristic had no exclusion which evaluated top 10 algorithms in DM which had its powerful principle that determines a query pattern based on repeated KNN class distribution in testing steps. Although, KNN was misled during problems that occurred in imbalanced classification problems since, KNN was dominated with patterns with negative classes and KNN was misled during imbalance problem and the negative patterns was dominated by query pattern so was the reason for selecting k in data-dependent and difficulty to tune.

The classes were unevenly distributed between classes that presented class imbalance in the dataset. The MLA community integrally disposed to imbalance class, motivating the amount of attention increased among many applications. The fact of learning algorithms created class imbalance in the data performed that created severity. The positive type comes for all the minority elements, whereas negative type comes for all majority elements. Internally, equal class distributions performed standard classification techniques that do not function well in context as they accept equal class distributions among classes. K. Jiang, J. Lu, and K. Xia, [23] developed a novel method called as Genetic Algorithm-based SMOTE (GA-SMOTE). Instances of certain minority classes used distinctive testing rates and ideal examining rates were determined for combined GA-SMOTE method. The practical application like rock burst in VCR rock burst was designed and developed a safe deep mining engineering structures and the paper included all these techniques. The application scope and practicability of these developed indexes were limited as it was very difficult to measure exactly or to calculate the strength based on the theory stress criteria and criterion of energy.

S. S. Mullick, S. Datta, and S. Das [24] developed a strategy called Adaptive KNN (Ada-KNN) for class imbalance in increasing the implementation of KNN classifier. The dissemination and the thickness of the test point neighborhood was point – explicit k for classification in assistance with artificial neural systems. The heuristic learning technique was replaced with neural system that indicated the thickness of the neighborhood test point that was used as a strategy. The strategy now was used as a replacing factor for neural system with heuristic learning technique with an indicator. The straightforwardness of KNN caused computational problem in weight that preserved the characteristics of developed method that was called as Ada-kNN2. To compensate the imbalanced data, class-based Global Weighting Scheme (Global Imbalance Handling Scheme or GIHS) was introduced. The method developed a distinct measure that influenced on the execution of Ada-KNN and Ada-KNN2 that depended on distinctive measure influences.

Y. Zhu, Z. Wang, and D. Gao [25] developed a novel model over the Gravitational Fixed Radius NN (GFRNN) methodology. The GFRNN strategy of execution of work on classification issues imbalanced on datasets. Usually, GFRNN does not possess any manual test parameters in entire procedure. FRNN rule uses GFRNN firstly that require manual set parameters in the whole path of procedure. The procedure is as follows firstly, GFRNN chose the appropriate pattern for the candidate and determined the gravitational energy among the query designs of the candidate. The consequence of the experiment presumed powerful and fundamentally basic NN learning proposed methods that deal with imbalanced acknowledgment assignment tasks effectively and automatically. Although, GFRNN spent extra time there impacted complexity on size of dataset where FRNN is a dataset dependent.

Y. Xu, Y. Zhang, J. Zhao, Z. Yang, and X. Pan, [26] developed KNN based Maximum Margin and Minimum Volume Hyper-sphere machine (KNN-M3VHM) of two hyper-Spheres even though it contained many samples. The samples of two classes continue as the maximum margin standard among two classes and also the edge between two classes continues. The results proved that the developed method techniques worked with all the existing techniques for almost all cases. The developed method resulted lowest value of accuracy when there were no preprocessed strategies techniques in the developed method. Meanwhile, the overall last decade produced a significant amount of work that has been developed in the imbalance problem. The custom classification process develops work at some approaches for data level. Modification in the training dataset produced sampling methods that modified to produce a balance between classes. The solutions for the existing methods modified accordingly with the intrinsic challenges obtained during imbalanced data classification. The large training datasets were simplified for prototype reduction techniques to remove noise tolerance and speed the leaning model requirements. The imbalanced datasets were applied to data level approach that balances the minority and majority classes. The two major prototype reduction techniques belonged to two families were applied to imbalanced datasets. The two major prototype reduction techniques that executed in literature are Prototype Generation (PG) and Prototype Selection (PS). The original training dataset selects for limited former for selecting the subset of instances whereas, the latter created a new artificial instances so as to adjust decision boundaries of classes. However, PG methods are known as susceptible to overfitting. The evolutionary based techniques performed best models such as differential evolution.

Selecting a subset of instances from that of original training data from limited former, whereas, the latter created a new artificial instances to adjust for better decision boundaries of the classes. However, these PG methods are suspected to be overfitting methods. The evolutionary techniques were based on the better performance of models. S. Vluymans, I. Triguero, C. Cornelis, Y. Saeys, [27] developed a hybrid strategy to exclusively organized with imbalance of class so called as Evolutionary Prototype Reduction Based Ensemble for NN Imbalanced Data (EPRENNID). To overcome overfitting of training dataset, the method performed EPR that provided distinct solutions. The additional technique permitted procedure to decrease the under-represented class, which was widely predicted as preprocessing for classifying the imbalance in the class. The outcomes obtained from classifying the imbalance in class resulted various set of models that were used in an ensemble that played weighted voting scheme with NN classifier. EPRENNID resulted extraordinary performance than the existing methods. EPRENNID resulted a better classification time that is marginally higher than other models which was due to the ensemble of specific weight of target construction for prototype sets. The preprocessing step resulted in certain model sets that were used again in an ensemble playing voting scheme with NN classifier. The EPRENNID has resulted much higher classification rate of time than other models which was due to specific weight construction of target that constructed prototype sets in the ensemble.

Survey on Review of Fuzzy Based Method on Imbalanced Dataset

A powerful classification was used for powerful approach that acquired sufficient exploration in MLA. Using the labeled training data and some classifiers the supervised learning method was prepared by some classifiers and finds the class name of test data. NN, Decision Trees, SVM, Bayes Classifiers etc., are some of the known classifiers that used the information of training data that fund the test data value of unknown. The prior information cases are not available or the rare samples that found classes for unknown test data. An efficient classification method which obtained information with prior was not available or samples that are usual to represent the data spaces, for efficient classification that was used in KNN. There was no presence of classifier that has preprocessed in absence and assigning of class label was done by utilizing distances between KNN and test data. The information regarding the membership of an instance grouped into classes with Fuzzy nearest neighbor. The more exactness obtained from classification results instead of benefits, the approaches provided the information regarding the instance of information into classes. The classification of results is known prior that neighbor set solutions that provided information of classes in an instance.

The neighbors of test instance prior to attain accurate classification resulted that strongly belonged to class. No random assignment is performed by the algorithm.

J. A. Sanz, et al., [28] developed an evolutionary interval-valued fuzzy rule-based classification system with Rule Selection and Tuning, was based on IVTURSFARC-HD, for prediction and modeling of applications in the real-world financially. Accuracies with good predictions were achieved in using proposed system allowed for attaining good accuracy values predictions for accuracies utilizing a small set of short fuzzy rules generated linguistic model implying a high degree of interpretability. Moreover, the imbalanced financial datasets were developed system with no need for any sampling method or preprocessing thereby, avoiding the unintentional overview of noise in the data used in the process of learning. The generated financial markets updated and generated financial models.

B. Krawczyk, et al., [29] introduced an effective cost-sensitive decision for ensemble trees for imbalanced classification. Base classifiers were given based on cost matrix that constructed, but were basically trained on subspaces of random feature to ensure ensemble members with sufficient diversity. The method employed an evolutionary algorithm for selection of simultaneous classifier and member weights were assigned of committee for the fusion process. The classification based on cost-sensitive classification was the major issues in the derivation of cost-matrices. But, this approach addressed based on analysis called as ROC, and presented that there existed a direct correlation between the imbalanced ratio of dataset and optimal cost matrix settings, and hence to signify an effective and useful approach for dealing with imbalanced datasets. The proposed method provided poor performance when there was a more extreme imbalance ratio.

Harshita Patel, and G. S. Thakur, [30] improved fuzzy K-NN classification of data that is imbalanced data that used the concept of adaptive KNN. Different values of K are arranged according to their sizes that facilitates changes in different values of classes. The advantage of adapting KNN of minority class which acquired better accurate data instances with accurate simple fuzzy K-NN for all the datasets. Better performance on imbalanced data was presented from the results. The results showed better performance of this algorithm on imbalanced data. This work was designed for binary classification and based on the quantity of NN. However, the method provides poor performance while having the imbalance data in feature-based NN for multi-label applications. M. Ohsaki, et al., [31] developed a Confusion-Matrix-based Kernel LOGistic Regression (CM-KLOGR) for classification performance by forming the dataset without task dependence and heuristics. Based on Minimum Classification Error and Generalized Probabilistic Descent (MCE/GPD) learning, the optimization and the objective function of CM-KLOGR were consistently formulated on KLOGR. The benchmark for imbalanced datasets were conducted which resulted more effectively CM-KLOGR method when compared with that of traditional techniques. Those methods had some drawbacks like task dependent and heuristic process due to cost-sensitive of ensemble methods.

Survey on Ensembles for the Class Imbalance Problem

The imbalance data of class refers as one for at least of classes is frequently that is outnumbered by different classes. The estimation wide variety of real-world domains like age estimation of facial age estimation detected oil spills from images of satellite, anomaly detection, fraudulent credit card transactions, image annotation and software defect prediction. The most popular methods of solving imbalance in problems that occurred during sampling was one of the important that eliminated the majority instances of classes or by increasing the instances of minority class. The class imbalanced problems are solved during sampling class imbalance problems has reported to occur across a wide variety of real-world domains, such as detecting oil spills from satellite images, facial age estimation, anomaly detection, identifying fraudulent credit card transactions, software defect prediction, and image annotation. Sampling is one of the most widely held methods for resolving the problems in class imbalance sampling. However, the original distribution of class with imbalanced data was eliminated by instances of majority classes, or increase in the minority class instances that were over-sampled and under-sampled. To solve the class imbalance problems, cost-sensitive learning was employed to solve. The misclassification errors under distinct classes effect on low rate of cost for majority class and the minority class. The Bagging and Boosting methods are mostly used to solve the imbalanced problems. Generally, the ensembles of classifiers are there to improve the accuracy of single classifiers thereby combining efficient ones, even though all these learning techniques failed to solve the imbalance problem. The ensemble learning is designed specifically.

Z. Sun, et al., [32] proposed an ensemble approach, that initially converted into multiple balanced ones from an imbalanced data set and then built a new data based on particular ensemble rule. Different classes of data handling methods for imbalanced data that considered specific ensemble rule. Imbalance handling methods with different classes included three conventional sampling methods. They are described as conventional sampling methods, six bagging and boosting based ensemble methods, cost-sensitive learning methods. The proposed method showed, 46 imbalanced data sets that were dominant that executed superior to balance data handling methods during solving highly imbalanced problems. The value of constant in the developed method that consisted denominator value as constant during classification performance that is neglected and a random number with constant value was selected.

K. Napierała, and J. Stefanowski, [33] focused on functioning rule based classifiers learned by incorporating expert knowledge into the learning process from class imbalanced data. The aim of the process was to present the functions of argument based learning to understand rules from imbalanced data. To attain the aim, a method was presented for a new argument rule based on ABMODLEM induction algorithm that is specialized only for categorization of classes explained by experts. From the results, the argument based learning improved minority recognition of class, exclusively for difficult data distributions with frequent examples and outliers. The SMOTE preprocessing and classifier with standard rule of classifier was distinguished by using ABMODLEM. The main drawback that novel proposed methods were identified with examples and examined by an expert. The argument based results showed better learning minority recognition of class especially for data distributions with complications with rare examples and outliers. Moreover, the standard rule classifiers and extensions with preprocessing with SMOTE was compared with ABMODLEM. The limitation with argument based learning was universally less with fully automated system improved the classifiers as per the knowledge of experts which was not available always or the acquisition of cost was too expensive. As per the knowledge, it was time consuming than other approaches and was limited in the scenarios that responded faster.

Y. Park, and Joydeep Ghosh, [34] presented two types of decision tree that accompanies imbalanced classification problems, extensively utilizing properties of α-divergence. A novel criterion of splitting tree was used in CART and C4.5. The splitting of α-divergence was applied to data with imbalance that obtained decision trees that was less correlated (α-diversification) by changing the value. At first, the diversity was increased in an ensemble trees that improved by trees like AUROC values, through a range of minority priors among classes. The second ensemble was used by the same alpha trees were based on classifiers. The obtained results from ensemble produced a set of interpretable rules that provided lift values with higher value for a given coverage, a property in applications of direct marketing. The datasets were provided effectively to imbalance the class datasets that provides effectiveness over a wide range of distribution of data and imbalance of class. The required number of trees reduced the different α-Tree rules that were not reduced by determining the relationships that simplifies LEAT output.

Summary

Classification of data is a hard task if the data is undergone overlapping or if the data is imbalanced. In the recent years, more focus is on the classification of imbalanced data because of the data omitted in the real world. During the classification, conventional methods are more successful with class that has the most samples termed as majority class and also compared to the other classes as minority classes. Thus the classification of imbalanced data sets has different methods, even though each has some merits and demerits. The authors have described a novel hierarchical decomposition method for data with imbalance which is unique from previously proposed solutions to the imbalance problem among classes.

Class overlapping has been considered the toughest problems in classification. When class overlapping is combined with class imbalance problem, the situation becomes even more complex. There are five widely used classifiers and class modeling schemes with three overlapping are activated for the comparative study. Given its importance and difficulty, in the literature, great research efforts have been dedicated to the class overlapping problem. The problem of multi-class imbalance and overlapping problems are presented by using Diversified Ensemble Classifiers (DEC) and clustering-based under sampling technique. The objective of DEC Algorithm is to provide an improved method for imbalanced data processing.

In this chapter, the theory and technology behind classification models is discussed briefly. This chapter also outlines a brief history of the different types of imbalanced techniques used for under-sampling and oversampling and discusses some most recent developments in this field. The chapter has also made mention of several advantages and disadvantages of imbalanced learning techniques of integrating with Artificial Intelligence. The chapter has also made mention of experimental frame work used for evaluation including algorithms used for comparison, validation technique, metrics used for evaluation and details of bench mark datasets used in the study. As a result of survey carried out for the research, the selected existing system for comparative analysis and improvise the performance in imbalance data set.

Chapter 3: Adaptive Condensed Nearest Neighbor for Imbalance Data Classification

The sample's size of one class is normally greater than that of other class is defined as the distribution of imbalanced data in real-world application scenario. The problems of class imbalanced distribution often present in various applications namely intrusion prevention, fraud detection, medical research and risk management. According to imbalanced dataset, classifiers are constructed which provides poor performance on minority class, whereas it performed well on majority class. When one class is often more interest and contains positive instance and other class is insufficiently represented are distributed in imbalance class dataset. In other words, number of samples from negative (majority) class is higher than the number of samples from positive (minority) class. When compared with one class, there exist are less number of instance in other class which leads to class imbalance problem. According to small size data in training set, the imbalance classification problem are also occurs due to insufficient data, which is considered as major challenging task in real-world applications.

In the following two important situations, the imbalance class distributions are occurred, which are stated as below:

- Intrinsic problems occur or it happens naturally, when the class is imbalance. Various difficulties are presents in class imbalance, which involves training sample size, small disjoints, distribution of imbalanced data and class overlapping.

- In each class, the overlapping patterns are exists in all features space or only in some features. The classes are separated by finding the discriminative rules, but it is very difficult to identify that rules [35, 36]. The good decision boundaries between classes are not identified easily due to loss of intrinsic properties in features, which are caused by overlapping feature space. These features are defined as irrelevant or redundant for recognizing the boundaries.

In this research work, ACNN algorithm is used for imbalance data classification. According to the pointer of class distributions and density of local neighborhood, a value of specific k information points are considered.In addition to the difficulty for finding the k, the characterization of KNN faces a provocations over the informational indexes with imbalance class, i.e., each class doesn't have an identical number of representatives.

Problem Statement

The decision systems are used for detecting the rare but important case of imbalance data, which is occurred in real-world applications domains. Nowadays, imbalance problems gained more interest among the committee of researchers. The significant problem statement of the research work is described below.

❖ In traditional KNN algorithm, the distribution of class and density of its local neighborhood are described by usingspecific data point k value. But, the data points of every classwas imbalanced and class indexes doesn't have an identical number hence, it's difficult to identify the classes.

❖ In learning process, the traditional imbalanced classification algorithms provide poor performance due to the distribution of uneven class samples. This shows that the classifiers achieved high precision on majority class and poor accuracy on minority class.

Contribution of the Research Work

In this section, the proposed imbalanced data classification research significant contribution is described below.

❖ ACNN method helps to reduce the difference between the data points to summarize the training set, finding the most important observations of information, which will be used to classify any imbalance data.

❖ The problem of non-linear regression is solved by specifying the data point values using feed-forward MLP with SCG learning algorithm for identifying the k -terrain. In the scales of small and medium datasets, the classifications are carried out by using the proposed ACNN algorithm.

Major Contests in Imbalanced Data

The class dispersion among classes in dataset isn't uniform, it is said to be an imbalance dataset [37]. In this condition, minority class represents at least one class in dataset, whereas majority class is described as rest of data in these dataset. In recent studies, the algorithms provide poor performance due to the presence of uneven distribution of class samples, which is used in learning process. In a majority class, this algorithm achieved very high precision values, but provides poor accuracy in a minority class. This shows that the general achievement of existing techniques gets highly affected by huge number of instances from dominant part class. In many real world problems, the minority classes play an important role for accurately classifying examples from this class [38]. The information balance issues are of two types namely binary and multi class data imbalance, which is recognized by various researchers.

When compared to other class, some classes are highly under-represented is known as class imbalance learning, which is one of the classification problems. A skewed distribution is generated with large amount of data in various real time applications [39]. Suppose, the one class contains higher number of samples than other class, then the dataset is described as highly skewed. Minor class contains less number of instances, whereas the major class consists of more instances in an imbalance dataset. The significant problems of imbalanced data components are described in the following sections.

Binary Class Imbalance Data

A class is represented by only a limited number of samples in a binary dataset are defined as imbalance problem for binary class data, which consists of only two classes. The two classes are separated in this dataset by using zero class thresholds. Hence, the boundaries of classes are no need to identify in dataset. The binary class imbalanced data is graphically shown in the Figure :3.1

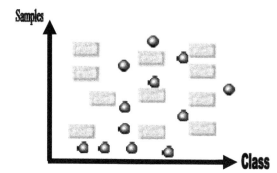

Figure 3.1: Binary Class Imbalanced Problems

In binary imbalanced classification, learning difficulties are not occurred only by imbalance ratio. A canonical classifieris used to achieve the good classification rates due to the well representation of classes and obtained from non-overlapping distributions, even though the disproportion is high. Specifically, in a minority class, the performance are degraded due to the presence of difficult samples, hence the relationship between classes are well defined as majority as one class and minority as other group [40]. Therefore, the shift classifiers or distribution towards minority class are balanced by using many straightforward approaches. The binary class imbalanced data classification process includes the several open challenges and it's described below.

- **Class Imbalance in an extreme Stage**

The disproportion between classes was considered as another important issue in binary imbalance data classification. The imbalance ratio in between 1:4 to 1:100 is the only concentrated ratios used in the existing contemporary works. But, still insufficient studies are presents in the classification for extreme imbalance datasets.

- **Adjustment in the output of Classifier**

In each classified objects, the output are adjusted by using the same parameter value of compensation for each class separately. There is a possibility of occurring an error in an majority class which will leads to overdriving the classifier towards minority class, which is the main drawback of methods depends on output adjustments. When the solutions of data- and algorithm-levels are previously used, these adjustments are used to modify the output, which is also known as independent approach. In this way, the refined classifiers are created to achieve balancing on various levels. The balanced performances on both classes are identified by analyzing the compensation of output which provides the supervising over-sampling or under-sampling.

- **Ensemble learning**

The combined majority voting techniques are used in most of the existing imbalanced ensemble learning methods, which is an effective and simple solution in standard scenarios. The individual qualities of base classifiers are varied because sampling methods are used to train these base classifiers. According to samples with various difficulties, the individual qualities may differ. When unknown samples are classified, the prediction of ensemble techniques are aggregated and multiple classifiers from the original data are constructed, which is the basic idea of ensemble learning classifier. An ensemble member includes training data, classifiers architecture, initial condition and training algorithm that are formed by manipulating numerous training parameters and factors. The training data (i.e., either input features or training set) are changed by most frequently ensemble methods. Figure :3.2 describes the general framework of ensemble learning method, which can alter the training data.

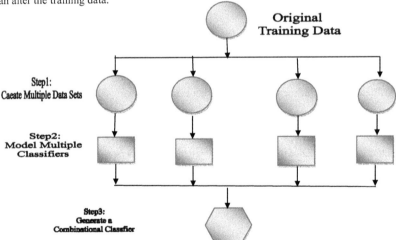

Figure 3.2: General Framework of Ensemble Learning Process

The ability to generalization is improved by combining the classifiers in redundant ensembles, which is the major aim of this learning technique. When the classifiers are trained on limited dataset, the errors are occurred by each component classifier. The various classifiers may misclassify the patterns, which are not necessarily the same. Under classification strategy, this observation recommends that the patterns recognition ability are improved by using multiple classifiers. The capability of overall recognition is enhanced by combining the set of imperfect estimators with limitations.

Multi Class Imbalance Data

Multi-class dataset are defined as the presence of more than two classes in a dataset, where extra overheads are occurred due to issues of information imbalance. The proficient zero class edge, which is a straightforward edge are unable to use as one of the part of this dataset. To address this kind of problem, techniques like Dynamic/Static Search Selection are introduced. The multiclass issue should have been partitioned into numerous paired class issues for sometimes to order the dataset. When compared with binary counterpart, this multi-class problem is not as much developed and also the relations between their classesare not obvious to deal with complex situation. When compared with other classes, a class is may be defined as majority class, and these other classes are called as minority or well-balanced class data [41, 42]. Figure 3.3: represents the graphical notation for this type of imbalance problem.

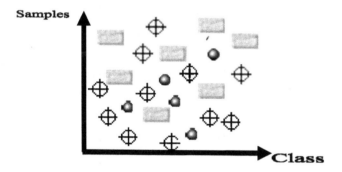

Figure 3.3: Multi Class Imbalanced Problems

The performances of one class are loss when trying to obtain from the other class while dealing with the imbalance data of multi-class problem. Numerous open challenges are present which requires a significant development for imbalanced learning from multi-label and instance data [43]. The multiple varieties of multi class imbalanced data samples are shown in the Figure 3.4.

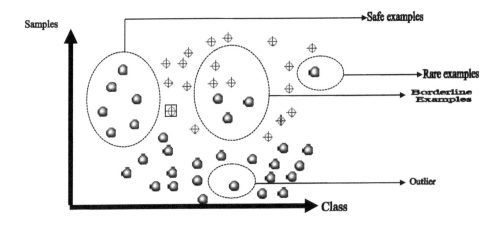

Figure 3.4: Presences of Various Samples in a Multi-Class Imbalanced Datasets

The multi-class includes different kinds of samples hence, its imbalance the dataset. The following samples are,

- Safe Examples: Examples those are correctly identified by the classifier.
- Outlier Examples: Present in the other class where it is treated as noise.
- Borderline Examples: Between various classes, there is a presence of boundary regions.
- Rare Examples: Small groups of examples that may consist of two or three examples.

The field of multi-label and instance imbalanced data faces challenges in learning, which are stated as follows:

- ❖ A skew-insensitive classifiers needs to develop in multi-label learning, because resampling techniques are not required in that classifiers. The combination of existing methods namely classifier chains or hierarchical multi-label classification with this skew classifier provides a solution in the domain of multi-class classification.
- ❖ Resampling bags are characterized by various uncertainty level in multi-instance learning, where bags consists of higher probability. The better representation of target concepts are carried out by objects that are presents in this resampling bags.
- ❖ The bags or objects within a bag are used in the current sampling approaches, but at same time, problems are occurred from both situations. Initially, the classifier performances are affected by which type of samples should be identified and also establish whether it is harmful to it.

Significant Strategies for Imbalanced Data

In various real world applications faces the problem in unbalanced dataset, where the applications includes detection of fault, fraud and oil-spills in satellite images, text categorization, medical diagnosis, toxicology and cultural modeling. Due to the distribution of unequal class, the existing classifiers performance provides poor performance towards minority class and achieved higher accuracy on majority class, which is proven by various researchers. The following main solutions are discussed below to address the imbalanced classification problem.

Sampling Methods

The problems with data distributions are solved by using sampling techniques, which consists of re-sampling the dataset artificially known as data pre-processing methods. The sampling techniques are achieved by two ways namely majority class is pre-processed by under-sampling, whereas the minority class is processed by over-sampling techniques [44, 45]. The classes are balanced by data level method that consists of resampling the original dataset. Approximately, the classes are equally represented by either under-sampling the majority class and over-sampling the minority class [46]. These strategies act as a pre-processing phase that are able to apply in any learning system for receiving training instance which are belongs to well-balanced dataset. There may be suppression in the performance of system towards to the majority class because of various proportions of samples per class. There are three types of sampling technique discussed in the below sections, which consists of oversampling, under sampling and hybrid methods.

Under samplingMethods

The imbalance learning is classified by under-sampling techniques, which is an efficient method and trains the classifier by using subset of majority class. The training sets are balanced to make the process faster by ignoring many majority classes in the imbalanced dataset. The under sampling method based majority sample removing process is graphically shown in the Figure 3.5.

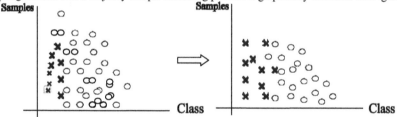

Figure 3.5: Random Removals of the Majority Samples

These sampling techniques are categorized into informative and random, where the majority class samples are randomly eliminated till balancing the dataset is known as random under-sampling techniques. According to pre-specified selection, only the required majority classes are selected by informative method for making the dataset balance. Furthermore, the informative sampling techniques are classified into two types, which are described as:

- The informative samples are selected for a classifier by using pre-processing techniques, also known as Passive selection methods [47].

- At the time of constructing the classifier, these informative samples are queried in active selection methods.

Among the above techniques, random-under sampling is the most common pre-processing to discard the majority classes from the dataset. These techniques neglect the useful information from these ignored samples and are considered as the major drawback of under-sampling techniques. Tomek Links, One-Sided Selection (OSS) and rules of CNN are proposed for improving the performance of random sampling. The noises or redundant of majority samples are intelligently removed by this OSS, which is proposed by Matwin and Rule Kubat [48].

Oversampling Methods

The class recognition of minority are improved by over-sampling methods, that duplicate the random minority data leads to overfitting problems. A small number of information for any category is not increased for duplicating these selected random data in over-sampling techniques. It makes a superset of the first informational index by duplicating a portion of the instances of the minority class, for instance by inserting the unique instances [49]. In over sampling, the replications of minority classes are shown in the Figure3.6.

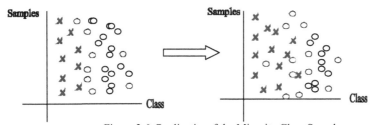

Figure 3.6: Replicationof the Minority Class Samples

The generation of classification rule is a common technique for a learner with oversampling methods for covering the samples of single and replicated. While increasing the number of training samples, it will automatically increase the learning time, which is also considered as the second disadvantage of over-sampling techniques. Here also like under-sampling, these techniques are categorized into two types, namely informative and random oversampling. The members from the minority class are selected randomly, duplicated and then added to the new training dataset by random over-sampling techniques. While using this technique, the researchers should notice two things, which are stated as:

- First major thing is that the researchers should collect the documents only from original training set, but not from the new training data set.
- The second is that researchers should always process the replacement randomly among the oversamples. Before reaching the desired balance between the classes of majority and

minority, the randomly selected samples without replacement will reduce the all minority class members.

Hybrid Methods

The advantages of properties of over-sampling and under-sampling are combined to form the hybrid in the sampling process. In other words, the outperforms of individual sampling methods are carried out by hybrid process, due to the controversy nature of under-sampling and over-sampling and solved the problem of skewed distribution in various extends [50]. It consolidates two above techniques by decreasing the measure of the larger part of the class and expands the quantity of minority component. The use of selected classifier for imbalance classification independently is the main advantage of information level techniques. An efficient sampling method is helps to handle the both oversampling or under sampling problems effectively. For example, the minority class new instances are created by using SMOTE techniques to form the neighboring instances of convex. Figure 3.7 is shows that minority points are monitored in feature space by SMOTE method, which is allows to balance dataset. A synthetic samples are newly created than duplicated samples by using this technique (i.e., SMOTE) to avoid the overfitting issues, but can't able to prevent every overfitting.

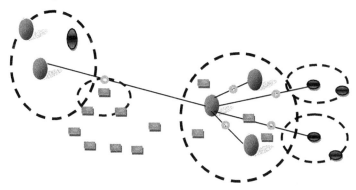

Figure 3.7: Visualization of SMOTE

Let consider that in minority class, x_i can be represented as each instance, where k nearest neighbors are searched by SMOTE and x' are randomly selected by one neighbor. For example, instances x_i and x' are seed samples. After that δ is generated by using the random number between the ranges of [0, 1]. Eq. (3.1) shows the creation of new artificial sample as x_{new}, are explained as below:

$$x_{new} = x_i + (x' - x_i) \times \delta \qquad (3.1)$$

The issues of overfitting are addressed by SMOTE method in an effective manner, when compared with random oversampling method [51]. The standard MLAs are influenced towards the majority class due to assumption of balanced distribution of class. The existing technique ignores the minority class and tries to optimize the overall accuracy of majority class distribution. Therefore, data imbalance in both algorithm and data-level should be deal by proposing the effective techniques, where resampling the data includes in data level solutions.

Structure of Explicit Algorithms

A class imbalance problem is solved by developing certain various new algorithms, which is used for optimizing the learning algorithm performance on unseen data. The samples of unseen data are identified by one-class learning methods, where other samples are rejected. In such conditions, multi-class dataset learning methods provides better performance than any another methods. The performance of classifier is improved by applying the cost for decision making, instead of changing the distribution of class.

Cost-Sensitive Learning Model

The misclassification costs or other type costs are taken into consideration by developing the CSL, which is a kind of DM techniques. The costs are minimized or profit is maximized by CSL which are associated with their decisions, when compared with methods for achieving high overall accuracy [52]. When compared with misclassifying samples of one class, the cost of misclassifying the samples of other class is very expensive. Therefore, the CSL techniques focused on the expensive misclassifying samples that are correctly predicted than treating all the classes equally. A loss function associated with dataset is maximized by using CSL techniques, which are motivated to find the real-world applications that are not having the uniform costs for misclassification. According to data, the cost matrix is identified by CSL methods to overcome the unknown errors which are associated with actual costs and then apply this cost matrix to the learning stage. The basic idea of CSL techniques are influenced by MLA techniques to consider the minority class in distribution of imbalance dataset.

The misclassification costs are same and it's assumed by the most classifier and this assumption is not always true in the various real-world applications. For instance, in medical domain, the misclassification of cancer would leads the patient's life in danger due to late diagnosis and treatment, which is considered very serious than false alarm. In this study, the cost is not an important factor, but it is a waste of time or not considering the severity of an illness. The CSL studies mainly focused to solve the problem of binary classification by representing the minority class as positive (+ or +1) and majority class as negative (− or −1). The cost matrix is defined in

Table 3.1, by considering the class i and j for predicting the cost for this class is represented as $C(i, j)$.

Table 0.1: Cost Matrix

Predicted classes	Actual class	
	Positive	Negative
Positive	C(+1, +1)	C(+1, -1)
Negative	C(-1, +1)	C(-1, -1)

The Bayes risk criterion (i.e., conditional risk) is used to construct the matrix with minimum expected cost by considering an example x that are classified into class i, which is shown in Eq. (3.2):

$$H(x) = arg \min_i (\sum_{j\in\{-,+\}} P(j|x)C(i,j))$$
(3.2)

Where, probability of posterior for classifying the sample x as j is represented from the Eq. (3.2) as $P(j|x)$. The cost matrix is described in Eq. (3.3) as cost matrix by assuming there is no cost for correct classifications.

$$CostRatio = C(-, +)/C(+, -)$$
(3.3)

Eq. (3.4) depicted the minimum misclassification rate which is used for building the model, that is the major purpose of CSL.

$$TotalCost = C(-, +) \times \#FN + C(+, -) \times \#FP$$
(3.4)

Where, the false negative numbers are depicted as $\#FN$ and false positive numbers are presented as $\#FP$. The function of misclassification cost adjustments are added into classifier and instance weights, then stacking ensembles are described by introducing the CSL to address the imbalance problem. The best distribution for training is selected by using the data space weighting as the misclassification costs in dataset. The standard cost-minimizing techniques are replaced by integrating the CSL with Meta techniques in the combine stage. The misclassification of positive instance weight is higher, whereas it is lower for the weight of negative instances. Hence, an option for imbalanced learning domain is provided by CSL [53].

Proposed Methodology

In various real-world datasets, classification faces the main issues known as unstructured class problem. When the minority class contains less number of instances than that of majority class then the dataset is defined as unstructured. Therefore, it provides poor performance of classification techniques. The unseen samples are classified by acquiring a training dataset using classification techniques, which is a part of supervised learning methods. When compared to standard accuracy or overall error rate, the common approaches are more sensitive to unbalance the distribution of class by improving training criteria or incorrect class predictions are assigned by various misclassification costs [54]. The normal classification accuracy of majority and minority classes are incorporated by enhanced learning criteria. The researcher proposes only limited strategy in a wide-ranging approaches, out of this well-known strategies is using the NN decision rule for accomplishing the issues of information imbalance. The Figure 3.8 demonstrates the basic structure of the model of ACNN.

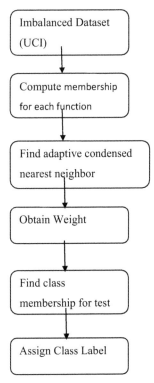

Figure 3.8: Basic Structure of the Proposed Method

Imbalance Dataset

A balanced dataset are acquired by resampling the training instances with specific goal in information level methodologies. This is can be achieved by using either minority class's over-sampling or majority class's under-sampling or hybrid techniques (i.e., combination of over- and under-sampling methods). The class imbalance issue is managed by such techniques, which is also known as pre-processing approach. According to dataset, the effects of such resampling techniques are applied on the classification task. In addition, the classification performances of unstructured data are influenced by selecting the wrong re-sampling techniques [55].

Computing Membership Function

While analysing about a classification issue and if the earlier probabilities and the state restrictive densities of all classes are known, the Bayesian decision hypothesis delivers the ideal outcome which reduces the expected misclassification rate [56]. Under this situation, numerous non-Bayesian grouping methods such as clustering and discriminant analysis describe the observations based on the notion of the distance or similarity in the feature space.The fuzzy set theory is combined with KNN algorithm as "fuzzy KNN classifier" (FKNN), which was proposed by Keller in 1985. His approach defined that the sample fuzzy memberships are assigned to various categories rather than the individual classes as in KNN are explained in Eq. (3.5):

$$u_i(x) = \frac{\sum_{j=1}^{k} u_{ij}(1/\|x - x_j\|^{2/(m-1)})}{\sum_{j=1}^{k}(1/\|x - x_j\|^{2/(m-1)})} \tag{3.5}$$

Whereas, number of classes and nearest neighbors are represented as C and k with $i = 1, 2, ..C$, and $j = 1, 2, .., k$. The weighted distance are identified by parameter of fuzzy as m and used to calculate the contribution of each neighbor to membershipvalue. By using this term $m \in (1, \infty)$, the selection process of weighted value are carried out. The distance between parameter x and its j^{th}nearest neighbor $x_j$is calculated by using the variable$\|x - x_j\|$. The definition for u_{ij} are carried out in two ways: crisp membership is a one way i.e., in a known class alone, each training pattern complete the membership, whereas in all other classes there is a non-memberships for that training pattern. When KNN distance are considered, membership degree are assigned to various classes, where in each class, a membership values are assigned to all the instances rather than binary decision of various classes [57]. The larger values are contributed to the data points, which is closer to the query points and the membership function are assigned to this larger values of the corresponding class when compared with far away neighbors. After computing membership function, the nearest neighbor values are forwarded to the ACNN classifier.

Nearest Neighbor Classification

An unclassified sample is assigned by decision rule of nearest neighbor classifier, which points the set of previously classified points for nearest classification. There is no need of underlying data distributions to explicit the knowledge for this decision rule. The probability of error for Bayes is twice bounded with probability of error for all distributions, which is considered as the strong point of this rule. The previously classified data are stored and compared the each classified sample point with each stored point, which is required for the Naive implementation of this rules. The nearest neighbor classifier also had limitations that it needs lot of memory space for storing all training patterns. The distance between every training pattern and query pattern q are computed to find the nearest neighbor of q and to classify the pattern of given query q. Therefore, consider $O(n)$ is the complexity of time, where n is the size of training set [58].

Among the influential DM algorithms, nearest neighbor is one of the top ten classifiers because of its high performance and simplicity. When the training instance is sufficiently large, this classifier error rate is not more than Bayes algorithm. The nearest neighbor classifier has no training phase without any priority knowledge of the query instance. But, also behaves like that the nearest neighbor is a prototype from the major class. The method provides poor performance for classifying the instances of minor class, especially when the minor instances are distributed between major ones [59].

Nearest Neighbor with Class Imbalance

In problems of classifications, the significant issues is the class imbalance, which are countermeasures namely CSL, instance-weighting, re-sampling are developed. Each and every approach contains its own advantage and limitations.

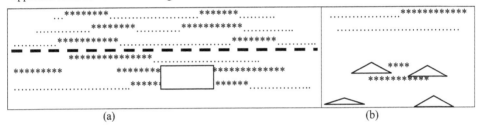

(a)   (b)

Figure 3.9: Nearest Neighbor Functions (a) Sample of Imbalanced Data (b) Decision Function of NN

An artificial dataset has a majority class, which are illustrated in the Figure 3.9, where the instances of minority and majority classes are indicated by red and blue dots. Figure 3.9 (a) shows the minority samples by rectangular region, whereas the Figure 3.9 (b) uses the red color shades to describes the minority samples and shows the nearest neighbor algorithms decision function that are reduced to Voronoi diagram over the magnified region. The majority class presence can induce type-II errors for a non-generalizing model as the nearest neighbor algorithm. The type-II errors occur with more precise of density estimation. The KDE using a smooth kernel function produces slightly smoother but similar decision boundaries as long as equal emphases are placed on the majority and minority estimation.

Class wise Nearest Neighbor Classification

The loss of non-linear performance is minimized by using the NN method over the imbalanced data is briefly described in this section. The importance of minority instanced are introduced to emphasize the non-parametric density model with weights are discussed. Secondly, the weight parameters learning problems are formulated from the training data is described. Then, the loss of non-linear NN performance is minimized which is considered as third procedure.

❖ **Weighted Density Model**

Consider the set of n points as X, where every point takes a value of class from $\{c_1, \ldots, c_m\}$. The centers of sphere are considered as x and contains the k instances for class c_i, also obtained the smallest radius for k instances of class as k-radius sphere of c_i. Therefore, $S_{i,k}(x)$ and $V_{i,k}(x)$ are used to define the sphere and its volume.

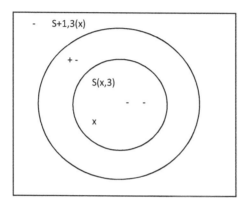

Figure 3.10: Class-Wise k-Radius Sphere

The imbalance data which contains the k-radius sphere are described in Figure 3.10, where the minority classes are represented as $\oplus$ and majority class instances are defined as $\ominus$. The original k-radius is indicated by dashed circle, whereas class-wise k-radius is described by solid circle. As explained in the above sample, majority instances of class-wise k-radius is smaller than that of minority instances. In the place of $V_{i,k}$, an adjusted k-radius is employed for compensation the sparseness of minority class. In Eq. (3.6), using β_i as positive coefficient, the adjusted volumes as $\tilde{V}_{i,k}$ is defined:

$$\tilde{V}_{i,k}(x) = \frac{1}{\beta_i} V_{i,k}(x) \tag{3.6}$$

For the majority class, k-radius is describes as the weight which is close to 1 and also similar to class-wise k-radius (i.e., sparseness of class is corresponds to the value β_i). In the meantime, set the β_i as larger value because k-radius of minority class is much smaller than the class-wise k-radius. According to the adjusted volume, membership function for posterior class is given in Eq. (3.7):

$$\hat{c} = \arg\max_i p(c \mid x) = \arg\max \frac{\beta_i}{V_{i,k}(x)} \tag{3.7}$$

The density of a point x is considered as $\tilde{V}_{i,k}$ and the distance to the KNN $D_k(x)$ are commonly approximated as $V_{i,k}(x)$. The above equation indicates the weighted k nearest neighbor. The procedure of new instance x in each class weighting function of NN algorithm is as follows.

❖ The training data $D_{i,k}(x)$ are used an approximation of $V_{i,k}(x)$, then the distance to the k-nearest instances are calculated for each class c_i.

❖ The Eq. (3.8) is used to calculate the maximum posterior as.

$$\hat{c} = \arg\max_{c_i} \frac{\beta_i}{D_{i,k}(x)} = \arg\min_{c_i} \frac{D_{i,k}(x)}{\beta_i} \tag{3.8}$$

According to weights set, the decision boundaries of minority class are expanded by using above equation.

❖ **Learning Structural Nearest Neighbor (SNN) classifier with nonlinear performance loss**

The SNN classifier is trained to optimize the quadratic programming problem which is formulated as non-linear performance measures are discussed in this section. This algorithm is extended to achieve the approximate solution for structural SVM learning. The binary classification problems are focused in this section for the sake of conciseness. It is similar, while addressing the intuition for more than one minority and majority classes because of its length.

Consider the training data as $(x_1, y_1) \dots (x_\eta, y_\eta)$, in that y obtains the class value from $\{-1, 1\}$. Sometimes, x can't be considered as a feature vector however, the representation of respective classes $d(x)$ is considered due to nearest neighbor distance. The equation $X = (d(x_1), \dots d(x_\eta))$ is described as input features, whereas the output is presented as $y = y_1 \dots y_\eta$ respectively. The decision function should formulate to optimize the loss of nonlinear performance, whereas, in each constraint of quadratic programming problem, all instances of input and output features are considered. Therefore, instance of multivariate output variable Y can be described as y and instance of multivariate input variable X are presented as x. Moreover, the losses in performances are measured by using the nonlinear associated with the loss function Δ to give an arbitrary prediction y', when compared with other given output y. The function of y and y' for Δ can be written as $\Delta(y, y')$. In Eq. (3.9), the definition for Ψ as feature function for the variables X and Y is given as below:

$$\psi(X, Y) = \sum_{i=1}^{\eta} y_i \begin{bmatrix} 1 & 0 \\ 0 & -1 \end{bmatrix} d(x)_i \tag{3.9}$$

In Eq. (3.10), the discriminant functions are described in a linear form:

$$f(X, Y; w) = < w, \psi(X, Y) > \tag{3.10}$$

Where, weight vector is described as $w = (\beta + 1, \beta - 1)$. The maximum margin with the decision function f provides the output as y in Eq. (3.11) and Eq. (3.12):

$$f(X; w) = \arg\max_{Y} F(X, Y; w) \tag{3.11}$$

$$f(X; w) = \arg \max \sum_{i=1}^{\eta} y_i (w^T d(x)_i) \qquad (3.12)$$

By decomposing the summation in Eq. (3.12) for each d, decision function for individual input are represented as f' is gained as

$$f'(X; w) = \arg \max_{y \in \{1,-1\}} y(w^T d) \qquad (3.13)$$

A quadratic programming problem are formulated by minimizing the loss Δ that are related to decision function in a linear process, which is shown in Eq. (3.13). While optimizing the weight parameters, the nearest neighbor weighted class obtains significant advantage as opposed for selecting the validated combined parameter values. In addition to this, the multiclass problems are handled by the capacity of ACNN algorithm which is explained in next section. The representation of extended distance feature on the class structure allowed the proposed method to exploit additional information [60].

Condensed Nearest Neighbor Algorithm

The whole sample needs to store, therefore large memory are required in KNN classifier, which is the main drawback of lazy learner (i.e., KNN). The response time on a sequential computer is large, when the number of samples in KNN is large. A parametric model is used to get rid the redundancy of training set and also decrease the number of free parameters, which is also considered as editing procedure. The subset of training set are stored for minimizing the number of stored patterns, that is the basic idea in training set and does not need any additional information, which can be discarded.

Let S be the sample subset, which can able to choose the best subset as represented by Z^* from the possible subsets. The error measure equation (3.14) is considered from the regularization theory.

$$Z^* = \arg \min_Z E(Z)$$

$$E(Z) = \sum_{x \in S} L(x|Z) + \gamma |Z|$$

$$\begin{cases} 1, & if\ D(Z_c, x) = min_j D(Z_j, x)\ and\ class(x) \neq clas(Z_c); \\ 0, & otherwise \end{cases} \qquad (3.14)$$

The variable $Z_c \in Z$ is the closest stored pattern to $x \in S$ using the distance measure D (.). Where, $L(x|Z)$ is non-zero when the labels of x and Z_c do not match. In the training set, when storing the subset classifiers, all the patterns are passing over the samples is sufficient, until no additions are required. The classification accuracy is increased at every pass and some patterns are included to the subset.

Pseudo code: Condensed Nearest Neighbor Algorithm

1. Procedure CNN (S, D, Z)
2. Start

3. $Z := \{\}$;

4. Repeat

5.   additions:=false;

6.   for all patterns in the training set Do

7.   From training set S, select the x randomly

8.   Find $Z_c \in Z$ such that $D(x, Z_c) = min_j D(x, Z_j)$

9.   If $class(x) \neq class(Z_c)$ Then

10. $Z := Z \cup x$;

11.   additions:=True

12.   end if

13.   end for

14. until not (additions);

15. end CNN

When compared with size (i.e., $\gamma < 1$), error is more important that is proven by the above pseudo code. When the order of training changes, the minimal subsets and various subsets are identifiedand which cannot be guaranteed by this method. In training set, when all patterns are classified by stored subsets until there is no additions are occurred and the samples are passed over few times is sufficient. The few patterns are included to the subset which increases the classification accuracy at each pass. There are two disadvantages presents in CNN namely unnecessary samples are preserved and the internal patterns are occasionally preserved rather than boundary patterns.

The CNN algorithm guarantees that all patterns in the training set will have the same classification with CNN and with the original classification set, and that the new set will not be larger than the original one. In practice, the classification set thus obtained, which we shall callCNN, is much smaller than the original set. While simple and reasonably efficient, this algorithm is far from optimal, and has a number of limitations.

➤ The first concern is the limitation. The final classification set, CNN, depends on the order by which the patterns are presented. Besides being annoying for many applications, this fact by itself shows that CNN will not find an absolute minimal classification set. In many cases the first prototypes to be added to CNN will later be made redundant, since prototypes closer to the border between the classes will inevitably be selected. The sensitivity to the order by which the patterns are presented may be partially overcome by re-initializing CNN with different permutations of the training set.

➤ The second concerns robustness no noise. Since all patterns in the training set will be classifiedexactly as they were in the original classification set, any outliers will be retained.

Since the CNNwill have fewer prototypes, those that remain will have greater importance, because we can no longer use the KNN algorithm to smooth out the outliers. Thus, the CNN method works best whenthe classes are separable.

Adaptive-Condensed Nearest Neighbor Algorithm

After computing the membership function, a semantic approach using ACNN approaches are utilized for identifying imbalance data. ACNN data reduction is used to summarize the training set, finding the most important observations of information, which will be used to classify any imbalance data. A new observation is automatically classified with slight accuracy reduction number of comparisons are reduced by the selection of ACNN data.

The manner in which the algorithm works is to isolate the information focuses into 3 different types:

- **Outliers:** Whenever points are added to the database, it cannot be considered as a right kind of data.

- **Prototypes:** In the training set, minimum set of points are required for many non-exception points that are observed effectively.

- **Absorbed points**: According to the prototype points set, the points that are not an anomalies are accurately observed.

At that point, the strategy needs to contrast imbalance information with the prototype points. The algorithm to do this can be outlined as:

1. Go through the preparation set, removing each point, and checking whether it is perceived as the right class or not. If the point, set it back in the set. Or if it is an outlier, and should not be returned.

2. Make another database, and include an arbitrary point.

3. Pick any point from the original set, and check whether it is perceived as the right class dependent on the point in the new database, utilizing KNN with $k = 1$. If the point is in recognized class, then it is an assimilated point, and can be let alone for the new database. If not, it ought to be expelled from the original set, and added to the new database of models.

4. Proceed through the original set this way.

5. Continue the steps 3 and 4, until no new modules are added in the point.

Since CNN has to keep repeating, this algorithm can take a long time to run [61]. The researchers solved the problem for improving the running time of this algorithm by using the extended techniques. However, when it has been run, the KNN calculation will be much quicker. CNN is also influenced by noise in the preparation set. In order to examine this, three informational indexes were created, and for everyone, the quantity of noise point was expanded, and CNN runs and record the level of points appointed to each type. As it can easily expand, the number of arbitrary noise points influenced the results of the CNN algorithm in three principle ways:

- The level of points classed as exceptions expanded drastically.
- The level of points classed as retained diminished.
- The level of points classed as prototypes expanded slightly.

These ways might be normal and the level of exceptions increases because of the fact that there are ever more noise points in each bunch, which will lead them to be misarranged. The level of points regarded as prototype increase because the data collection presently has a substantially more unpredictable structure once the data incorporated all these irregular noise points. The level of absorbed points in this manner must decline as the other two types are expanding (and the three are fundamentally unrelated).

Handling Imbalance in a Dataset

In class imbalance issues, the CNN classifier is proved to be efficient by using class specific weighted parameters. In the neighborhood of test point, the members of minority class are enlarged by using these class-specific weights, while reducing the majority classes for compensating their performance. A global class weighting scheme is used to weigh the classes and for all test points, it uses the same class weight. In class P, the representatives are equally distributed from each class, then according to class $c \in C$, the ideal probability of point should be $r = (1/C)$. The ratio of ideal and current probabilities are assigned by methods to have a better chance in the test point neighborhood for each class c as the global weight w_c, that are associated with this class are described in the Eq. (3.15), i.e.,

$$w_c = \frac{r}{p_c} \qquad (3.15)$$

Where, p_c is the prior probability of class c.

Assigning Class Label

With the ACNN calculation, class names of the k learning instances nearest to a testing instance, helps to decide the class name of the test example. Opposite separation weighting is to measure the vote of each neighbor as indicated by the backwardness of its separation from the test occurrence. By taking the weighted normal of the neighbors closest to the test instance smoothest out the effect of disconnected boisterous preparing occurrences. Besides, it lifts the heaviness of the instance.

Experimental Result and Discussion

When compared with existing classification techniques for imbalance data, the performance of ACNN are validated using various parameter metrics for benchmark datasets, which are having diverse nature are analyzed and discussed in this section.

Dataset Description

The extensive experiments are conducted on various standard datasets which is collected from the UCI machine learning repository. These datasets are able to download from the (http://archive.ics.uci.edu/ml/datasets.html). The imbalance dataset are obtained from the standard UCI datasets by randomly removing some negative or positive points. Here, the method used some of the UCI datasets such as Haberman, Pop-Failure, Cancer and Diabetes datasets are described below.

❖ **Haberman Dataset:**

This dataset collected data of the breast cancer patients from the Chicago's Billings Hospital at the time period of 1958 and 1970. There are several attributes in this dataset includes Age of the patient, operation year of patient, survival status and detection of positive auxiliary nodes. Suppose, if the patients survived for more than 5 years, the class status is described as 1 and 2 is given the class status, when the patients died within 5 years.

❖ **Pop-Failure Dataset:**

After failure detection on robot, this dataset consists of measurements in force and torque. At regular time intervals, each failure can be considered by 15 samples of force/torque that are started immediately after detecting the failure. The dataset are contains only integer values, but the features values are numeric. After failure detection, these features are described as a force or torque and each failure instance of total observation window time was 315 milliseconds.

❖ **Cancer**

The UCI database includes the several kinds of cancer dataset such as lung, brain, breast and etc. Here, randomly considers the imbalanced cancer data for experimental analysis. For example, one class of breast cancer dataset contains 201 instances, where these instances are defined by 9 attributes and another class consists of 85 instances. In 9 attributes, some are linear and some others are nominal.

According to the two following criteria, the data were collected from the database such as scale of the dataset and degree of imbalance. These two criteria are described below.

❖ **Scale of Dataset**

A data dimension greater than 45 along with a dataset contains more than 4000 data points as large-scale which is used in this paper. The other datasets are considered as scales of small and medium.

❖ **Degree of Imbalance**

The ratio of the number of points in the majority class with the minority class for a two class data set are defined, which can be quantified in the form of Imbalance Ratio (IR). The IR is taken to be the maximum values of IR calculated values between all the pairs of both minority and majority classes in the case of multi-class data sets. According to IR values, a data set can be classified as either balanced in the range of IR $\leq$ 1.15, mildly imbalanced between the range 1.15 < IR $\leq$ 3.5 or highly imbalanced for the value of IR is greater than 3.5. The Table 3.2 describes the six categories, where these dataset are presents in any one of these categories, which depends on above IR values

Table 3.2: Category of Dataset

Degree of Imbalance	Scale of Datasets	
	Small/Medium Scaled Datasets	Large Scaled Datasets
Balanced Datasets	Category 1	Category 2
Mildly Imbalanced Datasets	Category 3	Category 4
Highly Imbalanced Datasets	Category 5	Category 6

Evaluation Metrics

When compared with existing methods, the performance of the proposed ACNN performance are described in this experimental analysis in terms of Accuracy, Specificity, Positive Predictive Value (PPV), Negative Predictive Value (NPV), and Sensitivity. The estimation has been done for these parameters using TP, FP, FN, and TN values in which the calculation of parameters is described below:

- TP refers to True Positive,
- TN is True Negative,
- FP is False Positive and
- FN is False Negative

❖ **Accuracy**

Accuracy is the most instinctive execution measure and it is a proportion of effectively anticipated perception to the aggregate perceptions. The total results are directly proportional by considering both positives and negatives between the aggregate numbers of cases is defined by the accuracy metrics, where this parameter is measured in Eq. (3.16),

$$Accuracy = \frac{(TP+TN)}{(TP+TN+FP+FN)} \times 100 \qquad (3.16)$$

❖ **Specificity**

In a imbalanced dataset, the rules are obtained by the test, which have high specificity with positive results. The mathematical expression of specificity is in Eq. (3.17), which gives the negative proportion that is correctly identified.

$$Specificity = \frac{TN}{(TN+FP)} \qquad (3.17)$$

❖ **Sensitivity**

The sensitivity calculates the ratio of positives that are correctly recognized by samples. The mathematical equation of sensitivity is described in Eq. (3.18).

$$Sensitivity = \frac{TP}{(TP+FN)} \qquad (3.18)$$

The general formula for PPV and NPV are explained in following Eq. (3.19), (3.20)

$$PPV = \frac{TP}{TP+FP} \times 100 \qquad (3.19)$$

$$NPV = \frac{TN}{TN+FN} \times 100 \qquad (3.20)$$

Performance Analysis of Imbalanced Data Classification

In this section, the table.3.3 represents the performance of the proposed method in terms of accuracy, sensitivity, specificity, PPV and NPV for different datasets such as Diabetes, Cancer, Haberman and Pop failure. The traditional classifier is adjusted the data values to balance the classes. The proposed ACNN algorithm performed with respect to different imbalanced dataset. Table.3.3 shows the performance of the Diabetes dataset.

Table 3.3: ACNN Performance with Respect to Diabetes Dataset

ACNN classifier (k values)	Accuracy	Sensitivity	Specificity	PPV	NPV
20	83.8	80.1	76.6	79.5	80.6
40	89.1	85.4	87.4	84.2	84.3
60	91.8	89.8	90.5	89.7	89.9
80	92.9	91.9	96.3	93.7	95.2
100	93.2	89.3	92.7	96.1	90.1

The ACNN classifier performance with respect to Diabetes dataset is shown in the Table.3.3. The performance was measured using an efficient metrics such as accuracy, sensitivity, PPV and NPV. In classifier, the k value is varied such as 20, 40, 60, 80, and 100. In diabetes dataset, the data values in the classes are not balanced. But, the proposed ACNN classifier achieved approximately 93.2% of accuracy in imbalanced data classification. The graphical representation of diabetes dataset is shown in the Figure 3.11.

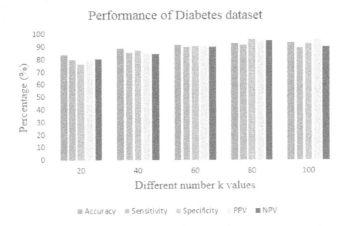

Performance of Diabetes dataset

Different number k values

■ Accuracy ■ Sensitivity ■ Specificity □ PPV ■ NPV

Figure 3.11: Performance of Diabetes Dataset

In Table.3.4, the proposed ACNN classifier performance with respect to cancer dataset is tabulated. The ACNN classifier helps to handle the large training samples efficiently with respect to different datasets. Moreover, if the training samples are noisy then also it is performing robustly. The ADCNN classifier includes the different k values and performance was depending on the k values. The significant advantage is simultaneously handles multiple imbalanced datasets. If the k values are increased, then the classification performance also increased. In this experimental analysis, the k values are varied up to 100. The proposed ACNN method achieved approximately 95.0% of accuracy in cancer dataset. The graphical representation is shown in the Figure 3.12.

Table 3.4: ACNN Performance with Respect to Cancer Dataset

ACNN classifier (k values)	Accuracy	Sensitivity	Specificity	PPV	NPV
20	86.2	82.4	86.7	79.8	82.3
40	89.1	89.7	89.1	84.6	87.4
60	92.8	92.4	91.3	89.1	90.7
80	94.7	94.9	92.6	92.7	92.3
100	95.0	95.58	93.10	96.58	93.10

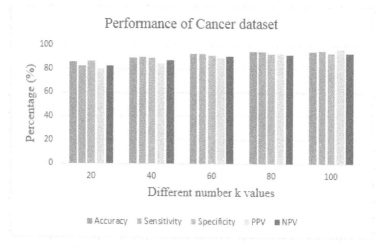

Figure 3.12: Performance of Cancer Dataset

Table 3.5: ACNN Performance with Respect to Haberman Dataset

ACNN classifier (k values)	Accuracy	Sensitivity	Specificity	PPV	NPV
20	75./	67.6	59.7	80.4	50.96
40	79.6	70.4	61.6	84.7	60.4
60	82.7	74.8	64.9	89.4	75.1
80	86.9	79.1	65.9	95.1	79.6
100	89.6	81	66.6	98.3	85.3

In Table.3.5, the proposed ACNN classifier performance with respect to Haberman dataset is tabulated. The performance measured using an efficient evaluation metrics such as accuracy, sensitivity, specificity, PPV and NPV in terms of different number of k values. If minority example exists in the neighbors, the local characteristic of the minority example will be analyzed to increase its weight. In the same way, we find out the distribution characteristics of the k values of the minority example, and calculate the number of the majority examples. The ACNN classifier achieved approximately 89.6% of accuracy, 81% of sensitivity, 66.6% of specificity, 98.3% of PPV and 85.3% of NPV. The graphical representation of the Haberman dataset performance is shown in the Figure 3.13.

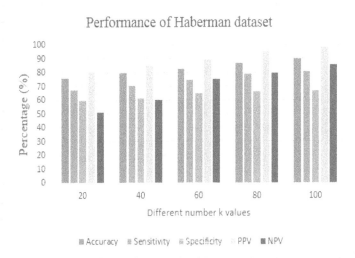

Figure 3.13: Performance of Haberman dataset

Table 3.6 ACNN Performance with Respect to Pop Failure Dataset

ACNN classifier (k values)	Accuracy	Sensitivity	Specificity	PPV	NPV
20	74.3	60.8	81.7	72.8	78.3
40	79.7	68.3	87.2	79.7	82.7
60	86.8	74.3	94.8	80.1	89.6
80	95.3	79.4	94.6	83.3	93.7
100	100	80.555	99.206	83.333	96.899

In Table 3.6 the ACNN classifier imbalanced data classification performance with respect to pop failure dataset. The proposed method increases the weight of minority class based on local characteristic of the minority class distribution. In addition to the imbalanced ratio, there may be other factors leading to the deterioration of the classification performance. The minority class does not form a uniform and compact distribution through the study of imbalanced datasets, but they are many small sub-clusters surrounded by a lot of majority class samples. In pop-failure dataset, the proposed ACNN classifier achieved 100% of accuracy, 80.5% of sensitivity, 99.2% of specificity, 83.3% of PPV and 96.8% of NPV. Compare to all the other datasets the proposed ACNN classifier shown better results in pop-failure dataset. The graphical representation is shown in the Figure 3.14, where the various numbers of k values are described in x-axis and percentage values for all metrics are presented in y-axis. Compare to all the dataset performance proposed ACNN method achieved 100% of classification accuracy because the dataset includes the minimum number of instances.

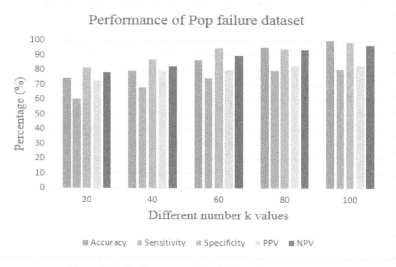

Figure 3.14: Performance of Pop-Failure Dataset

The graphical representation of the performance of various parameters is shown in Figure3.15. The ACNN achieved better consistency, scalability and best mean accuracy, which is proven by inspecting the results on small/medium scale dataset. The overall performance of ACNN method is tabulated in the Table 3.7.

Table 3.7: Overall Performance of ACNN Method

Dataset	Accuracy	Sensitivity	Specificity	PPV	NPV
Diabetes	93.2291	89.34426	45.714	74.149	71.11
Cancer	95.0	96.58	93.103	96.581	93.103
Haberman	89.6103	81.0810	66.66	98.36	12.5
Pop failure	100	55.555	99.206	83.333	96.899

The proposed ACNN achieved 96.581 PPV in Cancer dataset, but only 12.5 NPV in Haberman dataset. But, ACNN achieved 100% accuracy, but achieved only 55.55% sensitivity in pop-failure dataset. The proposed ACNN shows low average accuracy on large scale dataset, due to lack of k-terrain learning by underlying MLP which leads to various predictions of k_{y_i} values.

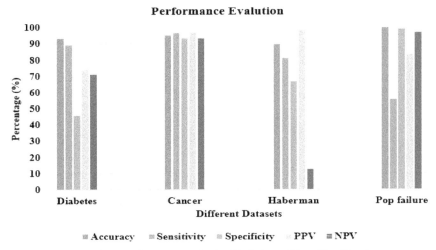

Figure 3.15: Performance Analysis of Imbalanced Data Classification

Comparative Analysis

In this area, the outcomes acquired by the ACNN are compared with CM-KLOGR [31], KLOGR [31], and SVM [31] discussed here. The Harmonic Mean (HM) of various parameters are extracted from a confusion matrix includes positive predictive values, sensitivity and others for negative, which is the main objective function of existing methods. According to the MCE/GPD learning, the framework of KLOGR formulates this objective function and its optimization. The accuracy of the existing method can be calculated from the HM of sensitivity, specificity and PPV. The performance of the ACNN for two datasets such as Haberman and pop-failure are discussed in Table 3.8.

Table 3.8: Performance of the Proposed Method

Datasets	Author	Methodology	Sensitivity	Specificity	PPV	HM
Haberman		CM-KLOGR	75	82.61	60	72.53
		KLOGR	75	78.26	54.55	69.27
		SVM	50	78.26	44.44	57.56
	Proposed	**ACNN**	**81.08**	**66.66**	**98.36**	**82.03**
Pop-Failure		CM-KLOGR	100	81.63	35.71	72.44
		KLOGR	100	93.88	62.50	85.46
		SVM	100	93.88	62.50	85.46
	Proposed	**ACNN**	**55.55**	**99.20**	**83.33**	**79.36**

When compared with existing techniques namely CM-KLOGR, KLOGR and SVM, the proposed ACNN achieved higher potential in all metrics, because it ranked the imbalanced classification data perfectly. The HM of the proposed achieved nearly 83% for Haberman dataset, but the ACNN achieved only 79.36% for pop-failure dataset. When compared to the existing methods like KLOGR and SVM for pop-failure, the ACNN method achieved less HM, this is because it leads poor performance in sensitivity. In many conditions, ACNN provides better performance than the existing methods with and without under/over-sampling methods, which is proved by above discussion. The HM of specificity, PPV and sensitivity are effectively increased by ACNN method. Therefore, from the experimental results, it is clearly shows that proposed ACNN are flexible and effective in all evaluation parameters such as PPV, NPV, sensitivity, specificity and accuracy.

Summary

In this section, summarizes the different key discoveries of the proposed technique and present the concluding comments. The classification of information over the traditional global decisions are carried out by adaptive decision of k values for the KNN classifier, (for example, if $k = 1$). The single global decision of k ignores such versatile decision obtained by ACNN, which is used to represent the test point properties of neighborhood. In IR, the execution of ACNN is very strong when compared with other traditional classifiers for imbalance data. While executing the ACNN the advantages is very clear those are briefly explained in this chapter. The extensive experiments are conducted on diabetes and pop-failure datasets showed that the proposed ACNN achieved 93.22% accuracy and 89.34% sensitivity for first datasets, whereas 100% of accuracy and 55.55% sensitivity for second dataset. The MLP-based ACNN faced the adaptability issues of large scale dataset because of choosing k values adaptively.

Chapter 4: Local Mahalanobis Distance Learning Based Imbalanced DataClassification

The patterns are extracted from the data is known as the process of DM. The associations of unsuspected data are identified by analyzing the observational dataset, which is useful and clear for data owner. By using this prevailing technology, the companies focus only on most important data that are collected from their data warehouses. The behaviors and future trends are predicted by the DM, which allows the business organizer for making knowledge-driven and proactive decisions, but one of the core tasks of the DM is the classification task. In training datasets or samples, when compared with one classes, the number of instances are higher than that of other classes is known as class imbalance problem. There are two categories presents in imbalance problem namely majority and minority class, where the number of instance are large in majority and small in minority classes. In general, the traditional classification algorithms are focused only on majority class and isolates the minority class, which leads to difficult for classification on imbalance dataset [62, 63]. A classifier completely ignores the minority class, which only predicts the sample from majority class is considered as class imbalance problem.

In classification problems, the data are presented as imbalance in various real-world applications includes IR, fault monitoring in helicopter, DM on direct marketing and medical diagnostic analysis. Therefore, researchers gained much interest on learning the classification from imbalance data [64]. The problem of data imbalance is overcome by resampling techniques such as over-sampling and under-sampling, but both sampling methods includes the several major limitations. The learning process is carried out by important information, but these data are potentially discarded by under-sampling technique. The training time is high because of large number of training instances at the time of learning process, which is caused by oversampling technique. During processing of data, training data suffers from high computational costs and provides inefficiency in memory, if a complex oversampling method is used. In this research work, when compared with traditional techniques, the proposed LMDL method based learning process preserves the distribution in original class. While decreasing the majority or increasing the minority, the proposed method didn't lose any information or may not cause unexpected mistakes. The input samples are reduced by considering the influence of neighborhood and multiple distance metrics are learned by LMDL. The local discriminative information ispreserved by these reduced set samples also known as prototypes. A set of various experiments are conducted to achieve the efficiency as well as quality of proposed LMDL method on various datasets. The significant problem statement and contribution of the research work is described in the following sections.

Problem Statement

Nowadays, the research community faces the main challenge is classifying the imbalance data. When data is imbalanced, the MLA behaves as one-sided classifier, where the significant problem statements are addressed below.

❖ A mapping process is strongly influenced due to presence of rare objects or noisy data in traditional kernel-based approaches, which is considered as a difficulty for individual instances.

❖ According to each class, there is no traditional learning systems performed effectively with huge variance between numbers of cases. When the data is imbalanced, classifiers are failed to fulfill the requirements of traditional systems.

The issues of small class problem are the separation of the small classes from the prevalent classes. Among each class, there is a presence of highly discriminative patterns, where no sophisticated rules are needed for differentiating the class objects. In some feature space, discriminative rules are difficult to induce, where the patterns among classes are overlapped at various levels.

Contributionof Research Work

In recent times, numerous existing methods are usedfor handle the imbalanced data classification. In this section, the significant contribution of the proposed LMDL method is addressed below.

❖ A LMDL is considered as a local distance metric learning method which is used for enhancing the performance of NN classifier. The LMDL learns the multiple distance metrics as well as influence the neighborhood for limited the input sample set.

❖ TheNearest Neighbor classifier use the AdaDelta rule to update the parameters for making the decision based on NN rules. It's an extension of AdaGrad rule and requires no manual tuning of the learning rate.

Nature of the Data Imbalanced Problem

The imbalance is formed in the dataset, where unequal distribution occurred between classes in any dataset. There are several categories presents in class imbalance problems, namely dataset complexity, relative imbalance, imbalance with small size dataset, imbalance based on rare instances, intrinsic and extrinsic [65].

Intrinsic and Extrinsic

In this category, an imbalance data which is directly related to the nature of the data space is referred as intrinsic, whereas the data are not related directly to data space nature is described as extrinsic. The intrinsic imbalance data may also occur due to various factors namely time and storage. As in the same line of intrinsic imbalance, the extrinsic also gain same research interests among the researcher community, because the extrinsic imbalanced dataset are occurred in the data space, where the data are not imbalanced at all.

Relative Imbalance and Rare Instances

The research engineering committee and various KDD focuses on relative imbalance, which may occur frequently in real-world applications. With little disturbance, the minority concepts are accurately learned from imbalance data for some relative imbalanced dataset, which is proven by few existing studies. An instance of minority classes are very limited (i.e., the concept of target is rare) is known as imbalance due to rare instances, which is a domain representative. With respect to the between-class imbalance, the learning process is very difficult due to insufficient representative data. In addition to this, the sub concept, with limited instances are present in minority concept, which leads to classifying the diverging degrees in a difficult manner.

Noisy Data

The predictive performance is affected, training time is increased and output of the classification model's complexity is also increased, due to presence of noise in data. From this, it is clear that the quality of training data and final model has strong correlation relationship. There are two major sources for the presence of noises in data is that measurement tools can introduce the errors and while gathering the data, experts may introduce random errors or by processing. According to the training set properties, data noises are classified into two types, namely, feature noise and label noise.

Label Noise: In the training set, when an object is provided with incorrect class label, label noise occurs. Due to several reasons includes data entry errors, insufficient data used for labeling each objects or subjectivity, class noise can be recognized. Two categories are presents in class label noise, which are discussed as:

- The different class labels are presents in duplicate objects, then there is a arise of contradictory objects;
- When compared with actual class, the mislabeled objects are assigned to another class.

Feature Noise: During data imputation, a machine or human may cause this type of noise (i.e., Feature Noise), for example, sensor/ measurement error [66]. The feature noise consists of different types such as,

- A measurement tools' quality or incorrect imputation causes erroneous feature values.
- Suppose, the requirement of specific attribute values from the given record is worthless or incorrect imputation leads to missing feature values.
- During record digitalization/archiving an incomplete features may appears or it may cause due to incorrect imputation.

The most common data quality problem is that of missing values. Despite greatefforts taken in data collection, data aggregated from multiple sources consists ofmissing values or unknown data, i.e., the value of attribute (s) is not present in the dataset. Table 4.1 shows that missing values symbolized by "?", are present in the attributes of A, D, and E of sample data.

Table 4.1: Missing Values in Sample Dataset

A	B	C	D	E	F	G	H	Class
6	148	72	35	?	33.6	0.62	50	Yes
1	85	66	29	?	26.6	0.35	31	No
8	183	64	?	?	23.3	0.67	32	Yes
1	89	66	23	94	28.1	0.16	23	No
?	137	40	35	168	43.1	2.28	33	Yes

In this sample dataset, the different attributes are indicated as A, B, C, D, E, F, G, and H. The classification states are yes and no. Here, the values are missed hence, the classification performance may have degraded but, classes of datasets are balanced.

Dataset Complexity

In addition to other problems, it is important to understand the dataset complexity. In classification deterioration, dataset complexity is the primary factor which is augmented by relative imbalance. An issue namely small disjoints, overlapping, noisy data, shortage of representative data are considered as data complexity, which is shown in Figure 4.1 [67]. In general the circles present the majority classes, whereas stars describe the minority classes in the sample figure.

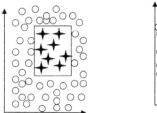 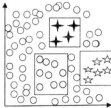

Figure 4.1: (i) Dataset with Less Imbalance Class (ii) Dataset with High-Complexity Imbalance class (i.e., noise, overlapping, insufficient representative data, etc).

By inspection, the paper explains both distributions in Figure4.1(i) and 4.1(ii) which contain relative imbalances. But, there is no overlapping between classes in Figure4.1(i), whereas the multiple concepts and severe overlaps are presents in Figure 4.1.(ii). The appearance of class imbalance problem are described as either inter class (occurs between classes) or intra class (occur within a single class). The large number of samples are present in one class than other class is defined as inter-class imbalance and their degree are calculated as the ratio of minority class size to majority class size. A various sub-concepts or sub-clusters are present in a class is defined as intra-class imbalance, and the number of samples are different in sub-clusters.

Imbalance with small size dataset: In this section the combination of small sample size problem and imbalance data are discussed. Nowadays, the analysis of KDD and data analytics faces the unavoidable issues like data with small sample size ad high dimensionality. In pattern recognition community, the traditional techniques considered only the small sample size problem. To handle these types of issues, dimensionality reduction methodologies are widely studies (i.e., Principal component analysis (PCA) and their extension methods). The combination of this problem paves new challenging issues for the research community, even though the imbalances forms are described earlier in the concept of representative dataset. There are two major issues are raised simultaneously in this concept as discussed below:

➤ First, absolute rarity and within-class imbalances are related to all issues presents in a small size samples, which are applicable.

➤ Final and important issue, when sample spaces are presents in this form of imbalance, inductive rules are generalized, which is considered as a difficult tasks for learning algorithms.

In this case, learning is hindered between the high-dimensionality and small sample size due to the formation of conjunctions with limited samples over the high degree of features. A set of albeit complex inductive rules are defined for the data space, when the sample space is sufficiently large. The problem of overfitting is occurred due to limited samples and the formation of rules also too specific. Therefore, the researchers should provide much proper attention to overcome these issues in regards to learning from such dataset.

Distance Learning Process in Imbalanced Data

In KDD and DM technology, the fundamental problem is the distance metric learning, where the DM techniques such as spectral, hierarchical clustering and KNN classifier to measure the relations correctly among input data that are highly relied on underlying distance metric. The performance of clustering, classification and retrieval tasks are improved by learning the good distance metric, which are shown in many studies either empirically or theoretically.

In the initial step, necessary concepts and notations are defined on the availability of various distance metric learning algorithms. The set of data points are indicated as X, if $x, y, z \in X$ are data vectors with the same dimensionality. The distance metric is represented as $D: X \times X \rightarrow \mathbb{R}$ and it satisfies the following properties.

Non-negativity: $D(x, y) \geq 0$

Coincidence: $D(x, y) = 0$ if and only if x=y

Symmetry: $D(x, y) = D(y, x)$

Subadditivity: $D(x, y) + D(x, y) \geq D(x, z)$

The coincidence condition to if $x = y \Rightarrow D(x, y) = 0$ then D is called Pseudo metric. The several distance metrics are defined below.

The distance between x and y are computed by using Euclidean distance, which is given in Eq.(4.1.)

$$D(x, y) = \sqrt{(x - y)^T (x - y)} \tag{4.1}$$

In addition, the distance between x and y are also calculated by using Cosine distance metric, that are described in Eq. (4.2)

$$D(x, y) = \sqrt{1 - \frac{x^T y}{\|x\|\|y\|}} \tag{4.2}$$

Where, in the above Eq.(4.2), the vector norm operator are represented as $\|.\|$. The pairwise documents distance is measured by using this cosine distance metric. Suppose, unit norm are obtained by normalizing the every data vector, then cosine distance can be similar to Euclidean distance. If the vector is zero, then cosine distance cannot able to define well, this shows that it is not a strict distance metric.

The distance between x and y are measure by $\chi 2$, which is given in Eq. (4.3)

$$D(x, y) = \sqrt{\frac{1}{2} \sum_{i=1}^{d} \frac{(x_i - y_i)^2}{x_i + y_i}} \tag{4.3}$$

Where, the dimensionality of x and y is described as d. The histograms i.e., distance between two discrete distributions are measured by using the distance metric known as $\chi 2$. This metric is also considered as non-strict distance metric, because two zero vectors are not well defined. But, often these existing learning approaches faces the computationally expensive problems.

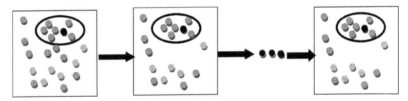

Figure 4.2: Examples for Finding a Stable Neighborhood Space for Testing Sample

The data space are modified by implementing an iterative metric learning, because only metric learning method is not able to provide efficient and stable neighbor for testing data, which is shown by Figure 4.2. By repeating the metric learning process for several times as in Figure4.2, the training data space is most related to testing data. According to testing data, most relevant data are selected by using sample selection process when the training data is unrelated and imbalanced. A subset of training data is located nearest to the testing data after the process of sample selection, which is used to construct the training data space. The issues of imbalance are solved in this step and the testing data are most relevant to training samples of neighborhood in this way. The structure of data space is modified by employing learning metric methods for improving the classification accuracy of imbalance data. The pairwise distances between samples from same class are minimized and samples are separated from the different classes using large margin, which is the objective of metric learning [68].

Significance of Nearest Neighbor Classifier in Imbalanced Data classification

According to other input attributes, the dependent variable set are estimated by classification, which is a kind of supervised learning approach. The process consists of two major steps i.e., building and testing the model. Various techniques such as decision trees, rule-based methods, neural networks etc are used for classification problem. According to numerous passes, the feasibility is explained over stored data, in which plenty of approaches are used to construct the various classification models from stationary datasets. There is no feasible in the case of data stream, because it contains infinite length, hence the whole data should proceed in a single pass [69]. When compared with samples of one/more class, the number of samples of another class is far in imbalance data stream, which are utilized in numerous real-world applications. In the field of data processing and MLA, class imbalance is the most important problem, because it reduces the overall accuracy as well as performance of DM techniques. The significant merits of NN classifier in imbalanced data classification is listed below.

➢ When compared to whole dataset, tuples in a locality have response variable values and the nearest neighbors are found by using this classifier. The variable of the predicted response values are more suitable, even though the tuples in locality are not considered as global nearest neighbors.

➢ If the classes are separable, the nearest neighbor rule converges to the true class, withprobability 1.If the classes are not separable, the nearest neighbor rule converges to an error rate that isless than twice the optimum Bayes error rate also with a probability of 1.

➢ The target labels are predicted using nearest neighbor classifier by finding their class. The distance measures like Euclidean distances are used to identify the closest class.

Preliminary Solution: KNN Strategy Based Imbalanced Data Classification

A classification decisions are considered by applying the intuitive and simple rule in KNN algorithm, where the input instance spaces are closely related to same class. Among the

KNN, the most frequently query instances are classified to class, where k is the tuning parameter for classification performance [70].

KNN algorithm bases onalogical learning, and supervised classifier. According to certain category in the feature space, the majority of a k most similar (i.e., the nearest neighbor) samples are also presents. The k nearest samples are find and locate the object into the most frequent category by KNN algorithm in the k samples. This algorithm only determines the target category according to the type of the nearest one or several samples. The decision-making rule is as below in Eq. (4.4.):

$$y' = \arg\max_{v} \sum_{(x_i, y_i) \in D_z} I(v = y_i) \tag{4.4}$$

In this function, v refers to the class label; y_i refers to the class label of a nearest neighbor; $I(\cdot)$ is the indicating function, if its parameter is true, returns 1, otherwise returns 0. The y' represents the value of v when $\sum_{(x_i, y_i) \in D_z} I(v = y_i)$ reaches the max value which also refers to the target category.

Nowadays, the distance between two samples in KNN algorithm are measured by using variety of distance functions. The Eq. (4.5) shows the Euclidean distance, which is used as a general function in KNN:

$$d(x', x) = [\sum_{i=1}^{n} (x_i' - x_i)^2]^{\frac{1}{2}} \tag{4.5}$$

In this function, $x' = (x'_1, x'_2, .. x'_n)$, $x = (x_1, x_2, .. x'_n)$, n refers to the dimensions of the input features. In KNN algorithm while $k = 1$, the target sample take the category of its nearest neighbor in the training set, this is also called the neighbor rule. The neighbor rule is simple and easy tooperate, and can obtain good performance in a large number of training samples. When $N \rightarrow \infty$, the classification error rate meets the following condition in Eq. (4.6):

$$P_B \leq P_{NN} \leq P_B \left(2 - \frac{M}{M-1} P_B\right) \leq 2P_B \tag{4.6}$$

P_B refer to the optimal Bayes error rate. When the optimal Bayes error rate is low enough, the approximation in following formulas is effective as in Eq.(4.7):

$$P_{NN} \approx 2P_B, P_{3NN} \approx P_B + 3(P_B)^2 \tag{4.7}$$

Therefore, when N large enough and the Bayes error rate is small enough relatively, the performance of $3 - NN$ classifier is very close to Bayes classifier. When the value of k increases, the similarity also increased.

In the class domains for various overlaps, when compared with other dataset, KNN is the most appropriate classifiers for large datasets due to its simplicity and easy for operations. The decision-making of algorithm didn't take advantage of other distance information, but it counts only on the information of training samples. However, the accuracy attains instability due to the choice of k values in the algorithms [71].Among the k-nearest prototypes, the most common label of training set are assigned as an input element in KNN classifiers. The major drawback of this classifier is that there is a low efficiency in memory usage and classification time due to the exhaustive search for each element [72]. Because of simplicity and easy implementation, KNN are considered as efficient and significant algorithm in DM. Generally, the traditional KNN algorithm includes the several limitations such as [73],

> ➤ The KNN algorithm is easy to implement but, when dataset size is increased then speed of the algorithm decline.
> ➤ The dimensionality of input samples are increased, which leads the prediction of the output for new data points are very difficult, even though KNN algorithm performs well in less number of input data.
> ➤ During the classification of new data entry the selection of optimal number of neighbors are the major issues with KNN.
> ➤ KNN inherently difficult to deal the missing values.
> ➤ The KNN classifier accuracy is highly depends on the distance metric performance.

Proposed Local Mahalanobis Distance Learning for Imbalance Data Classification

Keeping the similar samples closely together, while putting them far away from dissimilar points is the ultimate goal of the distance metric learning methods. The decision making process in NN algorithm is based on the way that distances are computed and hence, learning a proper distance metric can significantly improve the performance of this popular classification algorithm. To solve the complicated problems, Mahalanobis distance metric learning gained much interest because of its simplicity and efficiency, which is also known as global distance metric. The proposed imbalanced data classification is shown in the Figure4.3.

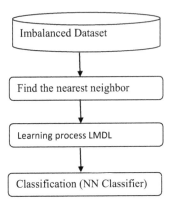

Figure 4.3: Proposed Imbalanced Data Classification Process

Learning Process Using LMDL

According to objective function which is closely related, a Mahalanobis distance metric are learned for each prototype, whereas a small set of samples (i.e., prototypes) is selected by LMDL in the initial step. Furthermore, the proposed learning procedure adjusts the prototype positions in order to minimize the objective function as well. Selecting prototypes mitigates the risk of overfitting while preserving the notion of locality. LMDL learns a Mahalanobis distance metric for each prototype. Moreover, our method is able to be used in kernel space as well.

Given a set of M training points, $x = \{(x^1, y^1), \ldots, (x^M, y^M)\}$, where $x^M \in \mathbb{R}^{d \times 1}$ and $y^m \in \{1,2, \ldots, K\}$ defines the corresponding class label, the ultimate goal is to learn a set of Mahalanobis metrics $W = \{W\}_{s=1}^s$ where $W^s \in \mathbb{R}^{d \times d}$ is a positive semi-definite matrix and corresponds to the sth member of a set of randomly selected prototypes $P = \{(p^1, y^1), \ldots, (p^s, y^s)\}$, $p^s \in \mathbb{R}^{d \times 1}$ and $S \ll M$. In this setting, vectors and matrices are respectively denoted by boldface lowercase and boldface uppercase letters. Accordingly, the scalars are denoted by uppercase or lowercase letters. Also, to have a compact representation of the parameters, suppose that $W \in \mathbb{R}^{(d \times d) \times s}$ is a matrix in which the sth column of W represents the vectorized form of W^s. Similarly, $P \in \mathbb{R}^{d \times s}$ is a matrix in which s^{th} column of P holds p^s and the ith column of $X \in \mathbb{R}^{d \times M}$ is the ith point in set X.

Using the above notations, the squared Mahalanobis distance between s^{th} prototype and i^{th} point in the input space is given by Eq. (4.8):

$$d^2_{w^s}(x^i, p^s) = \left\| x^i - p^s \right\|^2_{w^s} = (x^i - p^s)^T W^s (x^i - p^s) \tag{4.8}$$

Where, $W^s \in \mathbb{R}^{d \times d}_+$ is a symmetric Positive Semi-Definite (PSD) matrix and defined on the sth prototype. In order to minimize the error rate of the NN algorithm, the method use the following objective function which is a close approximation of the NN's error rate that is explained in Eq. (4.9)

$$J(W, P) = \frac{1}{M} \sum_{x^i \in X} \mathbb{S}_\beta (R(x^i)) \tag{4.9}$$

Where, $R(x^i) = \frac{d^2_{W^=}(x^i, P^=)}{d^2_{W^{\neq}}(x)}$ and $\mathbb{S}_\beta(z) = \frac{1}{1 - e^{\beta(1-z)}}$ is a sigmoid function and $P^=, P^{\neq} \in P$ are the nearest same-class and the nearest different-class prototypes of x^i is given in Eq. (4.10) and (4.11)

$$P^= = \begin{array}{c} argmin \\ p \in P \\ class(p) = class(x) \end{array} d^2_W = (x, p) \tag{4.10}$$

$$P^{\neq} = \begin{array}{c} argmin \\ p \in P \\ class(p) \neq class(x) \end{array} d^2_{w \neq}(x, p) \tag{4.11}$$

Accordingly, $W^=, W^{\neq} \in W$ are the corresponding Mahalanobis metrics of $P^=$ and $P^{\neq}$. The parameter β defines the slope of sigmoid function and if β is large, $\mathbb{S}_\beta(z)$ behaves like the step function more and more. Based on Eq. (4.9), the optimization problem can be written as follows:

$$(W^*, P^*) = \begin{array}{c} argmin \\ W \in \mathbb{R}^{(d \times d) \times S} \\ P \in \mathbb{R}^{d \times S} \end{array} J(W, P) \tag{4.12}$$

Which is, subjectto $W \geq 0, \forall W \in W$. Eq. (4.12), however, is a semi-definite programing with a non-convex objective function. Using the fact that $W \in W$ is a symmetric PSD matrix, which can be factorized as $W = WW^T$ where $W \in \mathbb{R}^{d \times p}$ and $p \leq d$. Hence Eq. (4.12) changes as Eq. (4.13),

$$(W^*, P^*) = \begin{array}{c} argmin \ (W \\ \widetilde{W} \in \mathbb{R}^{(d \times p) \times S} \\ P \in \mathbb{R}^{d \times S} \end{array} J(\widetilde{W}P) \tag{4.13}$$

Where s^{th} column of $W \in \mathbb{R}^{(d \times p) \times S}$ is the vectorized form of the matrix $\widetilde{W}^s \in \mathbb{R}^{d \times p}$.

Algorithm summarizes the proposed learning algorithm based on the above derivatives and similar to the learning procedure, which is an iterative gradient based procedure. Each iteration, $x \in X$ are visited by algorithm and updates those two metrics that have the highest impact in prediction of sample x and represent by $\tilde{W}^=$ and $W^{\neq}$. In other words, the algorithm updates $W^=$ in a way that nearest same-class prototype are closer to get the sample x, i.e., $P^=$, while updating $W^{\neq}$ in a way that it gets far from its nearest different-class prototype, i.e.,$P^{\neq}$. Concurrently the nearest prototypes for same and various-classes are modified in a way that $P^=$ moves towards x while $P^{\neq}$ gets away from x.

AdaDelta Method for Rule Generation

AdaDelta rule contains minimal computation overhead and uses only first order information beyond stochastic gradient descent, where it dynamically adapts over time. A learning rate tuning is not carried out by manual process and it behaves robust against different modalities, architecture choices, selection of hyper parameters and noisy gradient information. The two objectives are presented in the AdaDelta rule, which consists of the need of selection for global learning rate manually and there is a continuous learning rates delay throughout training.

The aggressive and learning rate is reduced by using AdaDelta, which is an extension of AdaGrad rule. The windows for accumulating the past gradients are restricted to some fixed size w instead of squaring all the accumulated past gradients. The decaying average of past squared gradients is recursively defined as gradients sum, instead of storing all previous gradients inefficiently. According to current gradient and previous average, the $E[g^2]_t$ as running average are described at time step t in Eq. (4.14):

$$E[g^2]_t = \gamma E[g^2]_{t-1} + (1-\gamma)g^2_t \qquad (4.14)$$

Where, constant delay is presented as γ, which is similarly used in the momentum method. In the parameter updates, this quantity are obtained by applying the square root, hence squared the previous gradients to time t, RMS are effectively obtained in Eq. (4.15):

$$RMS[g]_t = \sqrt{E[g^2]_t + \varepsilon} \qquad (4.15)$$

Where, a constant ε is added to better condition the denominator. The learning rate is indicated as η, which is indicated as $RMS[g]_{t-1}$. The Adadelta updatedrule is indicated in eq. (4.16):

$$\Delta x_t = -\frac{\eta}{RMS[g]_t} g_t \qquad (4.16)$$

The update rule eliminates the learning rate in AdaDelta hence there is no need to set the default learning rate. Momentum method is what incorporates momentum term into parameter update and the momentum term literally works as moment and helps update direction toward previously updated direction. Further, this method was modified to incorporate acceleration term. AdaGrad is adaptive method and it collects square of previousgradient information and based on the value, the learning rate is diminished gradually. The significant benefit of AdaDelta rule approach is listed below.

- A learning rate is not obtained by manual setting.
- The hyper parameters are not affected by rule (i.e., it is insensitive).
- The learning rate per dimension is separated based on its dynamic nature.
- The gradient descent is carried out by minimal computation.
- The AdaDelta are able to withstand the noise and more robust to architecture choice and large gradients.
- For both environments such as local or distributed, these rules are applicable.

AdaDelta rule is one of the best optimizers in current, which improved the performance of AdaGrad. The most basic idea of AdaDelta is incorporating a correction of mismatch of unit between update values and original parameters. The match of unit is naturally ensured by the second-order method like Newton method, though vanilla SGD, any other methods like AdaGrad basically do not have the system and it is the Alogorithm 1 which describes update rule of AdaDelta.

Pseudo code: Update the rule in AdaDelta

Requires: Objective function $f(\theta)$, Initial parameter θ_0, consider $\beta = 0.95$, $\varepsilon = 10^{-6}$

1. $v_0 = 0$, $s_0 = 0$, $h_0 = 0$
2. for $t = 0$: $t < T$ do
3. $g_t \leftarrow \nabla f(\theta_t)$
4. $v_{t+1} \leftarrow \beta v_t + (1 - \beta)g^2{}_t$
5. $s_{t+1} \leftarrow \beta s_t + (1 - \beta)h^2{}_t$
6. $h_{t+1} \leftarrow \frac{\sqrt{s_{t+1} + \varepsilon}}{\sqrt{v_{t+1} + \varepsilon}} g_t$
7. $\theta_{t+1} \leftarrow \theta_t - h_{t+1}$
8. end for
9. return θ_T

AdaDelta does not have the learning rate anymore. Here, ϵ is small value to avoid zero division and β is hyper parameter to control parameter update. In the context of unit correction, the most important variable is s. As shown in line 5, the unit of s corresponds to square root of h^2, namely parameter update h. Also, the unit of h is same as that of θ. Thus, there is no mismatch of unit between the update and parameters.

Algorithm for LMDL

//**Input**: X, S number of prototypes, β: slope of sigmoid, ε: small constant

//**Output**: $\tilde{W}$ P

   1. **Initialize** W & P randomly,

   2. **Set** $\tilde{W}^{ew} = \tilde{W} P^{new} = P, \lambda' = \infty, \lambda = J(\tilde{W}P)$

   3. **while**$(|\lambda' - \lambda| > \varepsilon)$ {

        3.1. $\lambda' = \lambda$

        3.2. **For** $x \in X$

                3.2.1. $P^{=} = findNNSameClass(x, P)$

                3.2.2. $P^{\neq} = findNNDiffClass(x, P)$

                3.2.3. $R(x) = d^2_{w=}(x, P^{=})/d^2_{w \neq}(x, P^{\neq})$

                3.2.4. Calculate $\nabla_{W=} J(\tilde{W}P), \nabla_{W \neq} J(\tilde{W}P), \nabla_{P=} J(\tilde{W}P), \nabla_{P \neq}(\tilde{W}P)$

                3.2.5. $[\alpha_{W=}, \alpha_{W \neq}, \alpha_{P=}, \alpha_{P \neq}] = Use \ theAdaDelta$ rule   to   find corresponding learning rate

                3.2.6. $\tilde{W}^{=,new} = \tilde{W}^{=} - \alpha_{W=} \odot \nabla_{W \neq} J(\tilde{W}P)$

                3.2.7. $\tilde{W}^{\neq,new} = \tilde{W}^{\neq} - \alpha_{W \neq} \odot \nabla_{W \neq} J(\tilde{W}P)$

                3.2.8. $P^{=,new} = P^{=} - \alpha_{P=} \odot \nabla_{P=} J(\tilde{W}P)$

                3.2.9. $P^{\neq,new} = P^{\neq} - \alpha_{P \neq} \odot \nabla_{P \neq} J(\tilde{W}P)$

        3.3. $\tilde{W} = \tilde{W}^{ew}$ & $P^{new} = P$

        3.4. $\lambda = J(\tilde{W}P)$

    In order to update parameters for making decision using NN rules, the method use AdaDelta rule which is an extension of AdaGrad rule and does not need the learning tuning rate by a manual process. When compared with various model architecture choices, hyper parameter selection, different data modalities and noisy gradient information, the AdaDelta shows robustness. During gradient descent's iteration, a good learning rate is estimated by using the heuristics for several attempts. The attempts are made on this iteration either to speed up or slow down the learning rate, which is near a local minimum. By decreasing the learning rate, the slow down for parameter updates are prevented by using AdaDelta technique. After the learning rate from this distance metrics, the rules can be identified by using NN for improving the accuracy of the proposed method.

Nearest Neighbor Based Imbalanced Data Classification

In various real-world applications, the classification problem is very hard due to presence of highly imbalanced datasets. According to the output of major classes, classifications of minor class instances are very difficult. The solution to this problem is the implementation of Nearest neighbor, which is the simplest and most popular classifier that provides better performance on various datasets. However, the correct minor class classification is sacrificed for achieving better performance when compared with others. Because of simplicity and higher performance, nearest neighbor is considered as one of top most influential DM algorithms. When the number of training instances are sufficiently large, the error rate of this algorithm are very less when compared with Bayes method for classification. There is no priority knowledge of query instances, so this classifier has no training phase and it seems like the nearest neighbor has prototype from majority class. In general, when there are minor instances are distributed in major ones; the performance of this classifier provides poor performance for classifying the instances of minor class. The detailed explanation is present in the section 3.5.3.

Experimental Result and Discussion

The influence of different methods for recognizing the minority and majority classes are validated and explained in this section, which is the main aim of extensive experiments. The performance of proposed LMDL method is validated from the collection of dataset that are having different nature by using standard metrics such as precision, recall, accuracy, which are described in this section.

Dataset Description

The data for experiments are collected from the standard UCI dataset, which is downloaded from the link (http://archive.ics.uci.edu/ml/datasets.html), which contains various numbers of samples, classes and dimensions. To get the imbalance dataset, randomly delete some negative points or positive points from the UCI datasets. Table 4.2 provides a brief summary of these datasets.

Table 4.2: Selected UCI Dataset for Proposed Method

Dataset	Samples	Dimensions	Classes
Iris	150	4	3
Breast Cancer	685	9	2
Wine	178	13	3
Diabetes	768	8	2
Glass	214	9	6
E-coli	336	7	5
Yeast	1484	8	3

The data collected from the dataset based on two criteria namely scale of dataset and degree of imbalance. If the data dimension is greater than 45 or the data points are more than 4000, the dataset is known as large-scale dataset. Other than this, all data can come under the category small/medium-scale and this paper used large-scale dataset for classifying the imbalance data. IR is used to evaluate the degree of imbalance, where the detailed descriptions are presented in the Section 3.6.1. The different datasets are defined below.

❖ **Iris Dataset:** There are 50 instances presents in 3 classes of Iris dataset, where one class is linearly separable and other two classes are not linearly separable from each other. In experimental analysis considers the 150 samples, 3 different classes and sample dimension is 4.

❖ **Breast cancer:** The University of Wisconsin Hospitals, Madison collected the breast cancer dataset from Dr. William H. Wolberg. The dataset contains 369 instances, but while conducting the experiments only 367 instances are used, where the other two are removed from Group 1. Here, missing attribute values are approximately 16. Here, consider the 685 samples, classes are 2, and attribute dimension is 9. The class distribution is Benign: 458 (65.5%) and Malignant: 241 (34.5%).

❖ **Wine:** In Italy, the chemical analysis results are defined as Wine data, which is derived from three cultivars but grown in same region. In each three types of wines, the quantities contain 13 attributes, which is obtained by this analysis. This dataset consists of 3 classes such as class1 includes 59 instances, class 2 includes 71 instances, and class 3 includes

48. There is no missing attribute values are presents in this dataset, whereas all the attributes are continuous.

❖ **Diabetes:** These data are collected from two sources such as paper records and automatic electronic recording device. In this dataset, 768 samples are available, 2 classes and the dimension value of each attribute is 9.

❖ **Glass:** This dataset includes 214 instances; the sample dimension is 9 and 6 different classes.

❖ **E-coli:** A rule-based system uses this version of dataset, but the results of this dataset are not-cross validated for classification purpose.It's includes the 336 instances, 5 different classes and each sample dimension value is 7.

Evaluation Measures

The performance of classification is measured by using traditional parameter i.e., accuracy, but it provides poor performance results on imbalanced dataset. Because of majority class instance, accuracy provides better results and often neglects the minority class instances. Therefore, other metrics such as F-measure, G-mean and AUC are used to validate the performance of LMDL technique, which shows better performance on imbalanced data for minority class instance. Table 4.3 shows the confusion matrix for validating the classifier on binary data.

Table 4.3: Confusion Matrix

	Predicted positive	**Predicted Negative**
Actual positive	TP	FP
Actual Negative	FN	TN

The actual positive instances are correctly classified as TP, whereas these positive instances are incorrectly classified as FP. Then, the negative instances are correctly classified as negative values (i.e., TN) and these instances are incorrectly classified as positive values (i.e., FN). All the majority classes are formed into a negative one by transforming the binary cases from multi-class problems. There are two kinds of measures are used by this method. First, precision, recall, TP rate and FP rate are defined as in Eq. (4.17-4.20)

$$Precision = \frac{TP}{TP+FP} \qquad (4.17)$$

$$Recall = \frac{TP}{TP+FN} \qquad (4.18)$$

$$TP_{rate} = \frac{TP}{Total\_P} \qquad (4.19)$$

$$FP_{rate} = \frac{FP}{Total\_N} \qquad (4.20)$$

The Eq. (4.21) defines the F-measure, which are combined by using all the above metrics are shown as:

$$F - Measure = \frac{2*Precision*Recall}{Precision+Recall} \qquad (4.21)$$

In various studies, G-mean is often used on imbalanced data, because mostly F-measure concentrates only on minority class. The trade-off can be shown between minority and majority class recognition using G-mean are described in Eq. (4.22)

$$G - Mean = \sqrt{recall \times precision} \qquad (4.22)$$

The AUC and Accuracy can be described in Eq. (4.23-4.24)

$$AUC = \frac{1+TP_{rate}-FP_{rate}}{2} \qquad (4.23)$$

$$Accuracy = \frac{TP+TN}{TP+FP+TN+FN} \qquad (4.24)$$

Summary

Nowadays, the performance of various real-world applications is affected by the uneven data distribution problem with imbalance data. Even though, the traditional classifiers such as NN, SVM, GA provides better performance in classification, they showed reduced performance when there is an available of imbalance data. The performance of KNN algorithm is enhanced by the proposed LMDL algorithm, where the similarity of local similar points of KNN is enlarged and also local dissimilar points are reduced as much as possible. The prototypes are defined as the reduced set of samples, which is obtained from multiple distance metrics. The neighborhood influence and these distance metrics are considered and learned by the proposed LMDL method. Each prototype has its own Mahalanobis metric trying to increase as much as possible the local discrimination. The prototypes position and their metrics are adjusted by objective function used by this method, which is closely related with error rate of NN. When compared with other existing techniques, this proposed method performed very good results, which is demonstrated by extensive experiments that are conducted on real-world and synthetic datasets. The results showed that the proposed LMDL method achieved nearly 98% in Iris Dataset, 93% in Breast cancer dataset, 80% in E-coli dataset for all metrics such as accuracy, precision, recall and F-Measure. The proposed LMDL provides poor classification performance in the case of highly nonlinear data.

Publisher: Eliva Press SRL

Email: info@elivapress.com

Eliva Press is an independent publishing house established for the publication and dissemination of academic works all over the world. Company provides high quality and professional service for all of our authors.

Our Services:
Free of charge, open-minded, eco-friendly, innovational.

-Free standard publishing services (manuscript review, step-by-step book preparation, publication, distribution, and marketing).
-No financial risk. The author is not obliged to pay any hidden fees for publication.
-Editors. Dedicated editors will assist step by step through the projects.
-Money paid to the author for every book sold. Up to 50% royalties guaranteed.
-ISBN (International Standard Book Number). We assign a unique ISBN to every Eliva Press book.
-Digital archive storage. Books will be available online for a long time. We don't need to have a stock of our titles. No unsold copies. Eliva Press uses environment friendly print on demand technology that limits the needs of publishing business. We care about environment and share these principles with our customers.
-Cover design. Cover art is designed by a professional designer.
-Worldwide distribution. We continue expanding our distribution channels to make sure that all readers have access to our books.

www.elivapress.com

www.ingramcontent.com/pod-product-compliance
Lightning Source LLC
Chambersburg PA
CBHW071551080326
40690CB00056B/1792